Library of
Davidson College

PREFACE
BY AMY LOWELL

LET me state at the outset that I know no Chinese. My duty in Mrs. Ayscough's and my joint collaboration has been to turn her literal translations into poems as near to the spirit of the originals as it was in my power to do. It has been a long and arduous task, but one which has amply repaid every hour spent upon it. To be suddenly introduced to a new and magnificent literature, not through the medium of the usual more or less accurate translation, but directly, as one might burrow it out for one's self with the aid of a dictionary, is an exciting and inspiring thing. The method we adopted made this possible, as I shall attempt to show. The study of Chinese is so difficult that it is a life-work in itself, so is the study of poetry. A sinologue has no time to learn how to write poetry; a poet has no time to learn how to read Chinese. Since neither of us pretended to any knowledge of the other's craft, our association has been a continually augmenting pleasure.

I was lucky indeed to approach Chinese poetry through such a medium. The translations I had previously read had given me nothing. Mrs. Ayscough has been to me the pathway to a new world. No one could be a more sympa-

PREFACE

thetic go-between for a poet and his translator, and Mrs. Ayscough was well-fitted for her task. She was born in Shanghai. Her father, who was engaged in business there, was a Canadian and her mother an American. She lived in China until she was eleven, when her parents returned to America in order that their children might finish their education in this country. It was then that I met her, so that our friendship is no new thing, but has persisted, in spite of distance, for more than thirty years, to ripen in the end into a partnership which is its culmination. Returning to China in her early twenties, she became engaged to an Englishman connected with a large British importing house in Shanghai, and on her marriage, which took place almost immediately, went back to China, where she has lived ever since. A diligent student of Chinese life and manners, she soon took up the difficult study of literary Chinese, and also accepted the position of honorary librarian of the library of the North China Branch of the Royal Asiatic Society. Of late years, she has delivered a number of lectures on Chinese subjects in China, Japan, America, and Canada, and has also found time to write various pamphlets on Chinese literature and customs.

In the Autumn of 1917, Mrs. Ayscough arrived in America on one of her periodic visits to this country. She brought with her a large collection of Chinese paintings for exhibition, and among these paintings were a number of

PREFACE

examples of the "Written Pictures." Of these, she had made some rough translations which she intended to use to illustrate her lectures. She brought them to me with a request that I put them into poetic shape. I was fascinated by the poems, and, as we talked them over, we realized that here was a field in which we should like to work. When she returned to China, it was agreed that we should make a volume of translations from the classic Chinese writers. Such translations were in the line of her usual work, and I was anxious to read the Chinese poets as nearly in the original as it was possible for me to do. At first, we hardly considered publication. Mrs. Ayscough lives in Shanghai and I in Boston, and the war-time mails were anything but expeditious, but an enthusiastic publisher kept constantly before us our ultimate, if remote, goal. Four years have passed, and after many unavoidable delays the book is finished. We have not done it all by correspondence. Mrs. Ayscough has come back to America several times during its preparation; but, whether together or apart, the plan on which we have worked has always been the same.

Very early in our studies, we realized that the component parts of the Chinese written character counted for more in the composition of poetry than has generally been recognized; that the poet chose one character rather than another which meant practically the same thing, because

PREFACE

of the descriptive allusion in the make-up of that particular character; that the poem was enriched precisely through this undercurrent of meaning in the structure of its characters. But not always — and here was the difficulty. Usually the character must be taken merely as the word it had been created to mean. It was a nice distinction, when to allow one's self the use of these character undercurrents, and when to leave them out of count entirely. But I would not have my readers suppose that I have changed or exaggerated the Chinese text. Such has not been the case. The analysis of characters has been employed very rarely, and only when the text seemed to lean on the allusion for an added vividness or zest. In only one case in the book have I permitted myself to use an adjective not inherent in the character with which I was dealing — and, in that case, the connotation was in the word itself, being descriptive of an architectural structure for which we have no equivalent — except in the "Written Pictures," where, as Mrs. Ayscough has stated in her Introduction, we allowed ourselves a somewhat freer treatment.

It has been necessary, of course, to acquire some knowledge of the laws of Chinese versification. But, equally of course, these rules could only serve to bring me into closer relations with the poems and the technical limits of the various forms. It was totally impossible to follow either the rhythms or the rhyme-schemes of the originals. All

PREFACE

that could be done was to let the English words fall into their natural rhythm and not attempt to handicap the exact word by introducing rhyme at all. This is the method I followed in my translations of French poems in my book, "Six French Poets." I hold that it is more important to reproduce the perfume of a poem than its metrical form, and no translation can possibly reproduce both.

Our plan of procedure was as follows: Mrs. Ayscough would first write out the poem in Chinese. Not in the Chinese characters, of course, but in transliteration. Opposite every word she put the various meanings of it which accorded with its place in the text, since I could not use a Chinese dictionary. She also gave the analyses of whatever characters seemed to her to require it. The lines were carefully indicated, and to these lines I have, as a rule, strictly adhered; the lines of the translations usually corresponding, therefore, with the lines of the originals. In the few poems in which the ordering of the lines has been changed, this has been done solely in the interest of cadence.

I had, in fact, four different means of approach to a poem. The Chinese text, for rhyme-scheme and rhythm; the dictionary meanings of the words; the analyses of characters; and, for the fourth, a careful paraphrase by Mrs. Ayscough, to which she added copious notes to acquaint me with all the allusions, historical, mythological, geographical, and technical, that she deemed it necessary for me to know.

PREFACE

Having done what I could with these materials, I sent the result to her, when she and her Chinese teacher carefully compared it with the original, and it was returned to me, either passed or commented upon, as the case might be. Some poems crossed continent and ocean many times in their course toward completion; others, more fortunate, satisfied at once. On Mrs. Ayscough's return to America this year, all the poems were submitted to a farther meticulous scrutiny, and I can only say that they are as near the originals as we could make them, and I hope they may give one quarter of the pleasure to our readers that they have to us in preparing them.

CONTENTS

INTRODUCTION   xix
LI T'AI–PO. (A.D. 701–762)
    Songs of the Marches   1
    Battle to the South of the City   5
    The Perils of the Shu Road   6
    Looking at the Moon After Rain   9
    The Lonely Wife   10
    The Pleasures Within the Palace   12
    The Young Girls of Yüeh   13
    Written in the Character of a Beautiful Woman   14
    Songs to the Peonies   16
    Spring Grief and Resentment   18
    The Palace Woman and the Dragon Robes   19
    The Nanking Wine-Shop   20
    Fêng Huang T'ai   21
    The Northern Flight   22
    Fighting to the South of the City   24
    The Crosswise River   26
    On Hearing the Buddhist Priest Play his Table-Lute   27
    Ch'ang Kan   28
    Sorrow During a Clear Autumn   30
    Poignant Grief During a Sunny Spring   32
    Two Poems Written to Ts'ui (the Official)   34
    Sent as a Parting Gift to the Second Official   35
    The Song of the White Clouds   36
    Wind-Bound at the New Forest Reach   37
    At the Ancestral Shrine of King Yao   38
    Drinking Alone in the Moonlight. I   39

CONTENTS

Drinking Alone in the Moonlight. II	40
Statement of Resolutions After Being Drunk	41
River Chant	42
Separated by Imperial Summons	44
A Woman Sings	46
The Palace Woman and the Soldiers' Cook	47
The Sorrel Horse	48
A Beautiful Woman Encountered on a Field-Path	49
Saying Good-Bye to a Friend	50
Descending the Extreme South Mountain	51
The Terraced Road	52
Hearing a Bamboo Flute in the City of Lo Yang	54
The Retreat of Hsieh Kung	55
A Traveller Comes to the Old Terrace of Su	56
The Rest-House on the Clear Wan River	57
Drinking Song	58
Answer to an Affectionate Invitation	60
Parrot Island	61
The Honourable Lady Chao	62
Thinking of the Frontier	63
A Song of Resentment	64
Picking Willow	66
Autumn River Song	67
Visiting the Taoist Priest	68
Reply to an Unrefined Person	69
Reciting Verses by Moonlight	70
Passing the Night at the White Heron Island	71
Ascending the Three Chasms	72
Parting from Yang, a Hill Man	73
Night Thoughts	74
The Serpent Mound	75
Old Tai's Wine-Shop	76
Drinking in the T'ao Pavilion	77

CONTENTS

Song for the Hour When the Crows Roost	78
Poem Sent to the Official Wang	79
Drinking Alone on the Rock in the River	80
A Farewell Banquet	81
Taking Leave of Tu Fu	82
The Moon Over the Mountain Pass	83
The Taking-Up of Arms	84
A Song of the Rest-House of Deep Trouble	85
The "Looking-For-Husband" Rock	86
After Being Separated for a Long Time	87
Bitter Jealousy in the Palace of the High Gate	88
Eternally Thinking of Each Other	89
Passionate Grief	91
Sung to the Air: "The Mantzǔ like an Idol"	92
At the Yellow Crane Tower.	93
In Deep Thought, Gazing at the Moon	94
Thoughts from a Thousand Li	95
Word-Pattern	96
The Heaven's Gate Mountains	97
On Hearing that Wang Ch'ang-ling Had Been Exiled	98
Parting Gift to Wang Lun	99
Saying Good-Bye to a Friend Going to the Plum-Flower Lake	100
A Poem Sent to Tu Fu	101
Bidding Good-Bye to Yin Shu	102

TU FU. (A.D. 712–770)

A Visit to the Fêng Hsien Temple	103
The Thatched House Unroofed by an Autumn Gale	104
The River Village	106
The Excursion	107
The Recruiting Officers	109
Crossing the Frontier. I	111
Crossing the Frontier. II	112

CONTENTS

The Sorceress Gorge	113
Thinking of Li Po on a Spring Day	114
At the Edge of Heaven	115
Sent to Li Po as a Gift	116
A Toast for Mêng Yün-ch'ing	117
Moon Night	118

PO CHÜ-I (A.D. 772–846)
    Hearing the Early Oriole   119

LIU YÜ-HSI (*Circa* A.D. 844)
    The City of Stones   120

NIU HSI-CHI. (*Circa* A.D. 733)
    Sung to the Tune of "The Unripe Hawthorn Berry"   121

WANG WEI. (A.D. 699–759)
    After an Imperial Audience   122
    The Blue-Green Stream   123
    Farm House on the Wei Stream   124

CH'IU WEI. (*Circa* A.D. 700)
    Seeking for the Hermit of the West Hill   125

CHI WU-CH'IEN. (*Circa* A.D. 733)
    Floating on the Pool of Jo Ya   126

MÊNG CHIAO. (*Circa* A.D. 790)
    Sung to the Air: "The Wanderer"   127

WEI YING-WU. (*Circa* A.D. 850)
    Farewell Words to the Daughter of Yang   128

WÊN T'ING-YÜN. (*Circa* A.D. 850)
    Sung to the Air: "Looking South"   130

DESCENDANT OF FOUNDER SOUTHERN T'ANG DYNASTY. (*Circa* A.D. 960)
    Together We Know Happiness   131

T'AO YÜAN-MING. (A.D. 365–427)
    Once More Fields and Gardens   132

CONTENTS

ANONYMOUS. LIANG DYNASTY (A.D. 502–557)
   Song of the Snapped Willow   134
AUTHORSHIP UNCERTAIN. CHOU DYNASTY.
REIGN OF KING HSÜAN. (826–781 B.C.)
   The Cloudy River   135
EMPEROR WU OF HAN. (156–87 B.C.)
   To the Air: "The Fallen Leaves"   139
EMPEROR CHAO OF HAN. (94–73 B.C.)
   Early Autumn at the Pool of Sprinkling Water   140
EMPEROR LING OF LATER HAN. (A.D. 156–189)
   Proclaiming the Joy of Certain Hours   141
PAN CHIEH-YÜ. (*Circa* 32 B.C.)
   Song of Grief   142
CHIANG TS'AI-P'IN. (*Circa* A.D. 750)
   Letter of Thanks for Precious Pearls   143
YANG KUEI-FEI. (*Circa* A.D. 750)
   Dancing   144
LIANG DYNASTY. (A.D. 502–557)
   Songs of the Courtesans   145
MOTHER OF THE LORD OF SUNG. (*Circa* 600 B.C.)
   The Great Ho River   147

WRITTEN PICTURES

An Evening Meeting   151
The Emperor's Return   152
Portrait of Beautiful Concubine   153
Calligraphy   154
The Palace Blossoms   155
One Goes a Journey   156
From the Straw Hut Among the Seven Peaks   157
On the Classic of the Hills and Sea   159

CONTENTS

The Hermit	160
After How Many Years	161
The Inn at the Mountain Pass	164
Li T'ai-po Meditates	165
Pair of Scrolls	166
Two Panels	167
The Return	168
Evening Calm	169
Fishing Picture	170
Spring. Summer. Autumn	171
NOTES.	173
KEY TO PLAN OF CHINESE HOUSE	223
TABLE OF CHINESE HISTORICAL PERIODS	227

Thanks are due to the editors of *The North American Review*, *The Bookman*, *The Dial*, *The New York Evening Post*, *Poetry*, and *Asia*, for permission to reprint poems which have already appeared in their magazines.

ILLUSTRATIONS

MAP *Frontispiece*

FACSIMILE OF " HANGING - ON - THE - WALL
   POEM " *To face p.* 170

PLAN OF CHINESE HOUSE *To face p.* 223

INTRODUCTION
By FLORENCE AYSCOUGH

THERE has probably never been a people in whose life poetry has played such a large part as it has done, and does, among the Chinese. The unbroken continuity of their history, throughout the whole of which records have been carefully kept, has resulted in the accumulation of a vast amount of material; and this material, literary as well as historical, remains available to-day for any one who wishes to study that branch of art which is the most faithful index to the thoughts and feelings of the "black-haired race," and which, besides, constitutes one of the finest literatures produced by any race the world has known.

To the confusion of the foreigner, however, Chinese poetry is so made up of suggestion and allusion that, without a knowledge of the backgrounds (I use the plural advisedly) from which it sprang, much of its meaning and not a little of its beauty is necessarily lost. Mr. Arthur Waley, in the preface to his "A Hundred and Seventy Chinese Poems," says: "Classical allusion, always the vice of Chinese poetry, finally destroyed it altogether." Granting the unhappy truth of this statement, the poetry of China is nevertheless so human and appealing as to speak with great force even

INTRODUCTION

to us who live under such totally different conditions; it seems worth while, therefore, to acquire a minimum of knowledge in regard to it and so increase the enjoyment to be derived from it. In the present collection, I have purposely included only those poems in which this national vice is less in evidence; and this was not a difficult task. There is such an enormous body of Chinese poetry that the difficulty has been, not what to take, but what to leave out. I have been guided somewhat by existing translations, not wishing to duplicate what has already been adequately done, when so much still remains untouched. Not that all these poems appear in English for the first time, but many of them do; and, except for Mr. Waley's admirable work, English renderings have usually failed to convey the flavour of the originals.

Chinese scholars rank their principal poets in the following order: Tu Fu, Li T'ai-po, and Po Chü-i. Realizing that, naturally, in any literature, it is the great poets which another nation wishes to read, I have purposely kept chiefly to them, and among them to Li T'ai-po, since his poems are of a universal lyricism. Also, Mr. Waley has devoted his energies largely to Po Chü-i. Tu Fu is very difficult to translate, and probably for that reason his work is seldom given in English collections of Chinese poems. Some of his simpler poems are included here, however. A small section of the book is devoted to what the Chinese

INTRODUCTION

call "written-on-the-wall-pictures." I shall come back to these later.

The great stumbling-block which confronts the translator at the outset is that the words he would naturally use often bring before the mind of the Occidental reader an entirely different scene to that actually described by the Oriental poet. The topography, the architecture, the fauna and flora, to say nothing of the social customs, are all alien to such a reader's own surroundings and cannot easily be visualized by him. Let me illustrate with a modern poem, for it is a curious fact that there has lately sprung up in America and England a type of poetry which is so closely allied to the Chinese in method and intention as to be very striking. This is the more remarkable since, at the time of its first appearance, there were practically no translations of Chinese poems which gave, except in a remote degree, the feeling of the originals. So exact, in fact, is this attitude toward the art of poetry among the particular group of poets to whom I have reference and the Chinese masters, that I have an almost perfect illustration of the complications of rendering which a translator runs up against by imagining this little poem of Miss Lowell's being suddenly presented to a Chinese scholar in his grass hut among the Seven Peaks:

INTRODUCTION

NOSTALGIA

By Amy Lowell

"Through pleasures and palaces" —
Through hotels, and Pullman cars, and steamships . . .

Pink and white camellias
    floating in a crystal bowl,
The sharp smell of firewood,
The scrape and rustle of a dog stretching himself
    on a hardwood floor,
And your voice, reading — reading —
    to the slow ticking of an old brass clock . . .

"Tickets, please!"
And I watch the man in front of me
Fumbling in fourteen pockets,
While the conductor balances his ticket-punch
Between his fingers.

As we read this poem, instantly pictures of American travel start before our eyes: rushing trains with plush-covered seats, negro porters in dust-grey suits, weary ticket-collectors; or marble-floored hotel entrances, clanging elevator doors, and hurrying bell-boys, also the vivid suggestion of a beautiful American house. But our scholar would see none of this. To him, a journey is undertaken, according to the part of the country in which he must travel, either in a boat, the types of which are infinitely varied, from the large, slow-going travelling barge capable of carrying many passengers, to the swifter, smaller craft

INTRODUCTION

which hold only two or three people; in one of the several kinds of carriages; in a wheelbarrow, a sedan chair, a mule litter, or on the back of an animal — horse, mule, or donkey, as the case may be. Again, there is no English-speaking person to whom "Home, Sweet Home" is not familiar; in a mental flash, we conclude the stanza suggested by the first line, and know, even without the title, that the subject of the poem is homesickness. Our scholar, naturally, knows nothing of the kind; the reference is no reference to him. He is completely at sea, with no clue as to the emotion the poem is intended to convey, and no understanding of the conditions it portrays. Poem after poem in Chinese is as full of the intimate detail of daily life, as dependent upon common literary experience, as this. There is an old Chinese song called "The Snapped Willow." It, too, refers to homesickness and allusions to it are very frequent, but how can an Occidental guess at their meaning unless he has been told? In this Introduction, therefore, I have endeavoured to give as much of the background of this Chinese poetry as seems to me important, and, since introductions are made to be skipped, it need detain no one to whom the facts are already known.

The vast country of China, extending from the plains of Mongolia on the North to the Gulf of Tonquin on the South, a distance of somewhat over eighteen hundred miles, and from the mountains of Tibet on the West to the

INTRODUCTION

Yellow Sea on the East, another stretch of about thirteen hundred miles, comprises within its "Eighteen Provinces" practically every climate and condition under which human beings can exist with comfort. A glance at the map will show the approximate positions of the ancient States which form the poetic background of China, and it will be noticed that, with the exception of Yüeh, they all abut either on the Huang Ho, better known as the Yellow River, or on the Yangtze Kiang. These two great rivers form the main arteries of China, and to them is largely due the character of the people and the type of their mythology.

The Yellow River, which in the old mythology was said to have its source in the Milky Way (in the native idiom, "Cloudy" or "Silver River"), really rises in the K'un Lun Mountains of Central Asia; from thence its course lies through the country supposed to have been the cradle of the Chinese race. It is constantly referred to in poetry, as is also its one considerable tributary, the Wei River, or "Wei Water," its literal name. The Yellow River is not navigable for important craft, and running as it does through sandy loess constantly changes its course with the most disastrous consequences.

The Yangtze Kiang, "Son of the Sea," often referred to as the "Great River," is very different in character. Its source lies among the mountains of the Tibetan border, where it is known as the "River of Golden Sand." After

INTRODUCTION

flowing due South for several hundred miles, it turns abruptly to the North and East, and, forcing its way through the immense wall of mountain which confronts it, "rushes with incredible speed" to the far-off Eastern Sea, forming in its course the Yangtze Gorges, of which the most famous are the San Hsia, or "Three Chasms." To these, the poets never tire of alluding, for, to quote Li T'ai-po, the cliffs rise to such a height that they seem to "press Green Heaven." The water is low during the Winter months, leaving many treacherous rocks and shoals uncovered, but rises to a seething flood during the Summer, when the Tibetan snows are melting. The river is then doubly dangerous, as even great pinnacles of rock are concealed by the whirling rapids. Near this point, the Serpent River, so-called from its tortuous configuration, winds its way through deep ravines and joins the main stream. As may be imagined, navigation on these stretches of the river is extremely perilous, and an ascent of the Upper Yangtze takes several months to perform since the boats must be hauled over the numerous rapids by men, called professionally "trackers," whose work is so strenuous that they are bent nearly double as they crawl along the towpaths made against the cliffs. In spite of the precipitous nature of the banks, many towns and villages are built upon them and rise tier on tier up the mountain sides. Having run about two-thirds of its course and reached the

INTRODUCTION

modern city of Hankow, the Great River changes its mood and continues on its way, immense and placid, forming the chief means of communication between the sea and Central China. The remarkably fertile country on either side is intersected by water-ways, natural and artificial, used instead of roads, which latter do not exist in the Yangtze Valley, their place being taken by paths, some of which are paved with stone and wide enough to accommodate two or three people abreast.

As travel has always been very popular, every conceivable form of water-borne craft has sprung up, and these the poets constantly used as they went from the capital to take up their official posts, or from the house of one patron to another, the ancient custom being for the rich to entertain and support men of letters with whom they "drank wine and recited verses," the pastime most dear to their hearts. The innumerable poems of farewell found among the works of all Chinese poets were usually written as parting gifts from the authors to their hosts.

As it nears the sea, the river makes a great sweep round Nanking and flows through what was once the State of Wu, now Kiangsu. This and the neighbouring States of Yüeh and Ch'u (the modern Chêkiang and parts of Hunan, Kweichow, and Kiangsi) is the country painted in such lovely, peaceful pictures by Li T'ai-po and his brother poets. The climate being mild, the willows which grow on the

INTRODUCTION

banks of the rivers and canals are seldom bare and begin to show the faint colour of Spring by the middle of January; and, before many days, the soft bud-sheaths, called by the Chinese "willow-snow," lie thick on the surface of the water. Plum-trees flower even while the rare snow-falls turn the ground white, and soon after the New Year, the moment when, according to the Chinese calendar, Spring "opens," the fields are pink with peach-bloom, and gold with rape-blossom, while the air is sweetly scented by the flowers of the beans sown the Autumn before. Walls and fences are unknown, only low ridges divide the various properties, and the little houses of the farmers are built closely together in groups, as a rule to the South of a bamboo copse which acts as a screen against the Northeast winds prevailing during the Winter; the aspect of the rich plain, which produces three crops a year, is therefore that of an immense garden, and the low, grey houses, with their heavy roofs, melt into the picture as do the blue-coated people who live in them. Life is very intimate and communistic, and the affairs of every one in the village are known to every one else. The silk industry being most important, mulberry-trees are grown in great numbers to provide the silk-worms with the leaves upon which they subsist, and are kept closely pollarded in order that they may produce as much foliage as possible.

This smiling country on the river-banks, and to the

INTRODUCTION

South, provides a striking contrast to those provinces lying farther North and West. Shantung, the birthplace of Confucius, is arid and filled with rocky, barren hills, and the provinces of Chili, Shansi, Shensi, and Kansu, which extend Westward, skirting the Great Wall, are also sandy and often parched for lack of water, while Szechwan, lying on the Tibetan border, although rich and well irrigated, is barred from the rest of China by tremendous mountain ranges difficult to pass. One range, called the "Mountains of the Two-Edged Sword," was, and is, especially famous. It formed an almost impassable barrier, and the great Chu Ko-liang, therefore, ordered that a roadway, of the kind generally known in China as *chan tao* (a road made of logs laid on piers driven into the face of a cliff and kept secure by mortar) be built, so that travellers from Shensi might be able to cross into Szechwan. This road is decribed by Li T'ai-po in a very beautiful poem, "The Terraced Road of the Two-Edged Sword Mountains."

These varied scenes among which the poets lived differed again from those which flashed before their mental eyes when their thoughts followed the soldiers to the far Northwest, to the country where the Hsiung Nu and other Mongol tribes lived, those Barbarians, as the Chinese called them, who perpetually menaced China with invasion, who, in the picturesque phraseology of the time, desired that their horses should "drink of the streams of the South."

INTRODUCTION

These Mongol hordes harassed the Chinese State from its earliest days; it was as a defence against them that the "First Emperor" erected the Great Wall, with a length of "ten thousand *li*" as Chinese hyperbole unblushingly states — its real length is fifteen hundred miles. This defence could, however, merely mitigate, not avert, the evil; only constant effort, constant fighting, could prevent the Mongol hordes from overrunning the country.

Beyond the Jade Pass in Kansu, through which the soldiers marched, lay the desert and the steppes stretching to the very "Edge of Heaven," and on this "edge" stood the "Heaven-high Hills"; while, on the way, surrounded by miles of sand, lay the Ch'ing Hai Lake (Green, or Inland, Sea), a dreary region at best, and peopled by the ghosts of countless soldiers who had fallen in battle on the "Yellow Sand Fields."

In addition to these backgrounds of reality, that of the Fertile Empire and that of the Barren Waste, there was another — that of the "Western Paradise" inhabited by the *Hsi Wang Mu* (Western Empress Mother) and those countless beings who, after a life in this world, had attained Immortality and dwelt among the *Hsien*, supernatural creatures living in this region of perfect happiness supposed to lie among the K'un Lun Mountains in Central Asia. From the spontaneous manner in which they constantly refer to it, and from the vividness of the pictures

INTRODUCTION

suggested by their references to it, one can almost question whether this Fairy World, the World of Imagination, with its inhabitants, were not as real to the writers of the early days as was the World of Actuality. Thus the topography of Chinese poetry may be said to fall into three main divisions, and allusions are made to

1. The beautiful scenes in the Eighteen Provinces.
2. The desolate region beyond the Jade Pass.
3. The glorious "Western Paradise."

Ideals determine government, and government determines social life, and social life, with all that the term connotes, is the essence of every literature.

The theory upon which the Chinese State was established is exceedingly interesting, and although the ideal was seldom reached, the system proved enduring and brought happiness to the people who lived under it.

The Emperor was regarded as the Son of the Celestial Ruler, as Father of his people, and was supposed to direct his Empire as a father should direct his children, never by the strong arm of force, but by loving precept and example. In theory, he held office only so long as peace and prosperity lasted, this beneficent state of things being considered a proof that the ruler's actions were in accordance with the decree of Heaven. Rebellion and disorder were an equal proof that the Son of Heaven had failed in his great

INTRODUCTION

mission; and, if wide-spread discontent continued, it was his duty to abdicate. The "divine right of kings" has never existed in China; its place has been taken by the people's right to rebellion.

This system created a very real democracy, which so struck the Dutchman, Van Braam, when he conducted a commercial embassy to the Court of Ch'ien Lung in 1794, that he dedicated his account of the embassy to "His Excellency George Washington, President of the United States," in the following remarkable manner:

Sir,
Travels among the most ancient people which now inhabits this globe, and which owes its long existence to the system which makes its chief the Father of the National Family, cannot appear under better auspices than those of the Great Man who was elected, by the universal suffrage of a new nation, to preside at the conquest of liberty, and in the establishment of a government in which everything bespeaks the love of the First Magistrate for the people. Permit me thus to address the homage of my veneration to the virtues, which in your Excellency, afford so striking a resemblance between Asia, and America. I cannot shew myself more worthy of the title of Citizen of the United States, which is become my adopted country, than by paying a just tribute to the Chief, whose principles and sentiments, are calculated to procure them a duration equal to that of the Chinese Empire.

The semi-divine person of the Emperor was also regarded as the "Sun" of the Empire, whose light should shine on high and low alike. His intelligence was compared to the penetrating rays of the sun, while that of the Empress found its counterpart in the soft, suffusing brilliance

INTRODUCTION

of the moon. In reading Chinese poetry, it is important to keep these similes in mind, as the poets constantly employ them; evil counsellors, for instance, are often referred to as "clouds which obscure the sun."

The Son of Heaven was assisted in the government of the country by a large body of officials, drawn from all classes of the people. How these officials were chosen, and what were their functions, will be stated presently. At the moment, we must take a cursory glance at Chinese history, since it is an ever-present subject of allusion in poetry.

Two favourite, and probably mythical, heroes, the Emperors Yao and Shun, who are supposed to have lived in the semi-legendary period two or three thousand years before the birth of Christ, have been held up ever since as shining examples of perfection. Shun chose as his successor a man who had shown such great engineering talent in draining the country, always in danger of floods from the swollen rivers, that the Chinese still say: "Without Yü, we should all have been fishes." Yü founded the first hereditary dynasty, called the Hsia Dynasty, and, since then, every time the family of the Emperor has changed, a new dynasty has been inaugurated, the name being chosen by its first Emperor. With Yü's accession to the throne in 2205 B.C., authentic Chinese history begins.

Several centuries later, when Yü's descendants had deteriorated and become effete, a virtuous noble named

INTRODUCTION

T'ang organized the first of those rebellions against bad government so characteristic of Chinese history. He was successful, and in his "Announcement to the Ten Thousand Districts," set forth what we should call his platform in these words: "The way of Heaven is to bless the good and punish the wicked. It sent down calamities upon the house of Hsia to make manifest its crimes. Therefore I, the little child, charged with the decree of Heaven and its bright terrors, did not dare forgive the criminal . . . It is given to me, the one man, to ensure harmony and tranquillity to your State and families; and now I know not whether I may not offend the Powers above and below. I am fearful and trembling lest I should fall into a deep abyss." The doctrine that Heaven sends calamity as a punishment for man's sin is referred to again and again in the ancient "Book of History" and "Book of Odes." It is a belief common to all primitive peoples, but in China it persisted until the present republic demolished the last of the long line of dynastic empires.

T'ang made a great and wise ruler. The Dynasty of Shang, which he founded, lasted until 1122 B.C., and was succeeded by that of Chou, the longest in the annals of Chinese history — so long, indeed, that historians divide it into three distinct periods. The first of these, "The Rise," ran from 1122 B.C. to 770 B.C.; the second, "The Age of Feudalism," endured until 500 B.C.; the third, "The

INTRODUCTION

Age of the Seven States," until 255 B.C. Starting under wise rulers, it gradually sank through others less competent until by 770 B.C. it was little more than a name. During the "Age of Feudalism," the numerous States were constantly at war, but eventually the strongest of them united in a group called the "Seven Masculine Powers" under the shadowy suzerainty of Chou. Although, from the political point of view, this period was full of unrest and gloom, from the intellectual it was exceedingly brilliant and is known as the "Age of Philosophers." The most famous names among the many teachers of the time are those of Lao Tzŭ, the founder of Taoism, and Confucius. To these men, China owes the two great schools of thought upon which her social system rests.

The "Age of the Seven States" (Masculine Powers) ended when Ch'in, one of their number, overcame and absorbed the rest. Its prince adopted the title of Shih Huang Ti, or "First Supreme Ruler," thus placing himself on an equality with Heaven. Is it to be wondered at that the scholars demurred? The literary class were in perpetual opposition to the Emperor, who finally lost patience with them altogether and decreed that all books relating to the past should be burnt, and that history should begin with him. This edict was executed with great severity, and many hundreds of the *literati* were buried alive. It is scarcely surprising, therefore, that the name of Shih Huang

INTRODUCTION

Ti is execrated, even to-day, by a nation whose love for the written word amounts to veneration.

Although he held learning of small account, this "First Emperor," to give him his bombastic title, was an enthusiastic promoter of public works, the most important of these being the Great Wall, which has served as an age-long bulwark against the nomadic tribes of Mongolia and Central Asia. These tribes were a terror to China for centuries. They were always raiding the border country, and threatening a descent on the fertile fields beyond the mountains. The history of China is one long struggle to keep from being overrun by these tribes. There is an exact analogy to this state of affairs in the case of Roman Britain, and the perpetual vigilance it was obliged to exercise to keep out the Picts.

Shih Huang Ti based his power on fear, and it is a curious commentary upon the fact that the Ch'in Dynasty came to an end in 206 B.C., shortly after his death, and only a scant half-century after he had founded it.

A few years of struggle, during which no Son of Heaven occupied the Dragon Throne, succeeded the fall of the Ch'in Dynasty; then a certain Liu Pang, an inconsiderable town officer, proved strong enough to seize what was no one's possession and made himself Emperor, thereby founding the Han Dynasty.

The Han is one of the most famous dynasties in Chinese

INTRODUCTION

history. An extraordinary revival of learning took place under the successive Emperors of Han. The greatest of them, Wu Ti (140–87 B.C.), is frequently mentioned by the poets. Learning always follows trade, as has often been demonstrated. During the Han Dynasty, which lasted until A.D. 221, intercourse with all the countries of the Near East became more general than ever before, and innumerable caravans wended their slow way across the trade routes of Central Asia. Expeditions against the harassing barbarians were undertaken, and for a time their power was scotched. It was under the Han that Buddhism was introduced from India, but deeply as this has influenced the life and thought of the Middle Kingdom, I am inclined to think that the importance of this influence has been exaggerated.

This period, and those immediately preceding it, form the poetic background of China. The ancient States, constantly referred to in the poems, do not correspond to the modern provinces. In order, therefore, to make their geographical positions clear, a map has been appended to this volume in which the modern names of the provinces and cities are printed in black ink and the ancient names in red. As these States did not all exist at the same moment, it is impossible to define their exact boundaries, but how strongly they were impressed upon the popular mind can be seen by the fact that, although they were merged into

INTRODUCTION

the Chinese Empire during the reign of Shih Huang Ti, literature continued to speak of them by their old names and, even to-day, writers often refer to them as though they were still separate entities. There were many States, but only those are given in the map which are alluded to in the poems published in this book. The names of a few of the old cities are also given, such as Chin Ling, the "Golden Mound" or "Sepulchre," and Ch'ang An, "Eternal Peace," for so many centuries the capital. Its present name is Hsi An-fu, and it was here that the Manchu Court took refuge during the Boxer madness of 1900.

Little more of Chinese history need be told. Following the Han, several dynasties held sway; there were divisions between the North and South and much shifting of power. At length, in A.D. 618, Li Shih-min established the T'ang Dynasty by placing his father on the throne, and the T'ang brought law and order to the suffering country.

This period is often called the Golden Age of Chinese Learning. The literary examinations introduced under the Han were perfected, poets and painters were encouraged, and strangers flocked to the Court at Ch'ang An. The reign of Ming Huang (A.D. 712–756), the "Brilliant Emperor," was the culmination of this remarkable era. China's three greatest poets, Li T'ai-po, Tu Fu, and Po Chü-i, all lived during his long reign of forty-five years. Auspiciously as this reign had begun, however, it ended sadly. The Em-

INTRODUCTION

peror, more amiable than perspicacious, fell into the toils of his favourite concubine, the lovely Yang Kuei-fei, to whom he was slavishly devoted. The account of their love story — a theme celebrated by poets, painters, and playwrights — will be found in the note to "Songs to the Peonies." A rebellion which broke out was crushed, but the soldiers refused to defend the cause of the Emperor until he had issued an order for the execution of Yang Kuei-fei, whom they believed to be responsible for the trouble. Broken-hearted, the Emperor complied, but from this date the glory of the dynasty was dimmed. Throughout its waning years, the shadow of the dreaded Tartars grew blacker and blacker, and finally, in A.D. 907, the T'ang Dynasty fell.

Later history need not concern us here, since most of the poems in this book were written during the T'ang period. Though these poems deal largely with what I have called the historical background, they deal still more largely with the social background and it is, above all, this social background which must be understood.

If the Emperor were the "Son of Heaven," he administered his Empire with the help of very human persons, the various officials, and these officials owed their positions, great and small, partly to the Emperor's attitude, it is true, but in far greater degree to their prowess in the literary examinations. An official of the first rank might owe his

INTRODUCTION

preferment to the Emperor's beneficence; but to reach an altitude where this beneficence could operate, he had to climb through all the lower grades, and this could only be done by successfully passing all the examinations, one after the other. The curious thing is that these examinations were purely literary. They consisted not only in knowing thoroughly the classics of the past, but in being able to recite long passages from them by heart, and with this was included the ability to write one's self, not merely in prose, but in poetry. Every one in office had to be, perforce, a poet. No one could hope to be the mayor of a town or the governor of a province unless he had attained a high proficiency in the art of poetry. This is brought strikingly home to us by the fact that one of the chief pastimes of educated men was to meet together for the purpose of playing various games all of which turned on the writing of verse.

The examinations which brought about this strange state of things were four. The first, which conferred the degree of *Hsiu Ts'ai*, "Flowering Talent," could be competed for only by those who had already passed two minor examinations, one in their district, and one in the department in which this district was situated. The *Hsiu Ts'ai* examinations were held twice every three years in the provincial capitals. There were various grades of the "Flowering Talent" degree, which is often translated as Bachelor of

INTRODUCTION

Arts, some of which could be bestowed through favour or acquired by purchase. The holders of it were entitled to wear a dress of blue silk, and in Chinese novels the hero is often spoken of as wearing this colour, by which readers are to understand that he is a clever young man already on the way to preferment.

The second degree, that of *Ch'ü Jên*, "Promoted Man," was obtained by passing the examinations which took place every third year in all the provincial capitals simultaneously. This degree enabled its recipients to hold office, but positions were not always to hand, and frequently "Promoted Men" had to wait long before being appointed to a post; also, the offices open to them were of the lesser grades, those who aspired to a higher rank had a farther road to travel. The dress which went with this degree was also of silk, but of a darker shade than that worn by "bachelors."

The third examination for the *Chin Shih*, or "Entered Scholar," degree was also held triennially, but at the national capital, and only those among the *Ch'ü Jên* who had not already taken office were eligible. The men so fortunate as to pass were allowed to place a tablet over the doors of their houses, and their particular dress was of violet silk.

The fourth, which really conferred an office rather than a degree, was bestowed on men who competed in a special examination held once in three years in the Emperor's Palace. Those who were successful in this last examination

INTRODUCTION

became automatically *Han Lin*, or members of the Imperial Academy, which, in the picturesque phraseology of China, was called the "Forest of Pencils." A member of the Academy held his position, a salaried one, for life, and the highest officials of the Empire were chosen from these Academicians.

This elaboration of degrees was only arrived at gradually. During the T'ang Dynasty, all the examinations were held at Ch'ang An. These four degrees of learning have often been translated as Bachelor of Arts, Master of Arts, Doctor of Literature, and Academician. The analogy is so far from close, however, that most modern sinologues prefer to render them indiscriminately, according to context, as student, scholar, and official.

By means of this remarkable system, which threw open the road to advancement to every man in the country capable of availing himself of it, new blood was continually brought to the top, as all who passed the various degrees became officials, expectant or in being, and of higher or lower grade according to the Chinese measure of ability. Military degrees corresponding to the civil were given; but, as these called for merely physical display, they were not highly esteemed.

Since only a few of the candidates for office passed the examinations successfully, a small army of highly educated men was dispersed throughout the country every three

INTRODUCTION

years. In the towns and villages they were regarded with the reverence universally paid to learning by the Chinese, and many became teachers to the rising generation in whom they cultivated a great respect for literature in general and poetry in particular.

The holders of degrees, on the other hand, entered at once upon a career as administrators. Prevented by an inexorable law — a law designed to make nepotism impossible — from holding office in their own province, they were constantly shifted from one part of the country to another, and this is a chief reason for the many poems of farewell that were written. The great desire of all officials was to remain at, or near, the Court, where the most brilliant brains of the Empire were assembled. As may be easily imagined, the intrigues and machinations employed to attain this end were many, with the result that deserving men often found themselves banished to posts on the desolate outskirts of the country where, far from congenial intercourse, they suffered a mental exile of the most complete description. Innumerable poems dealing with this sad state are found in all Chinese anthologies.

There were nine ranks of nobility. The higher officials took the rank of their various and succeeding offices, others were ennobled for signal services performed. These titles were not hereditary in the ordinary sense, but backwards, if I can so express it. The dead ancestors of a nobleman

INTRODUCTION

were accorded his rank, whatever had been theirs in life, but his sons and their descendants had only such titles as they themselves might earn.

The desire to bask in the rays of the Imperial Sun was shared by ambitious fathers who longed to have their daughters appear before the Emperor, and possibly make the fortune of the family by captivating the Imperial glance. This led to the most beautiful and talented young girls being sent to the Palace, where they often lived and died without ever being summoned before the Son of Heaven. Although numberless tragic poems have been written by these unfortunate ladies, many charming romances did actually take place, made possible by the custom of periodically dispersing the superfluous Palace women and marrying them to suitable husbands.

In striking contrast to the unfortunates who dragged out a purposeless life of idleness, was the lot of the beauty who had the good fortune to capture the Imperial fancy, and who, through her influence over the Dragon Throne, virtually ruled the Middle Kingdom. No extravagancies were too great for these exquisite creatures, and many dynasties have fallen through popular revolt against the excesses of Imperial concubines.

It would be quite erroneous to suppose, however, that the Emperor's life was entirely given up to pleasure and gaiety, or that it was chiefly passed in the beautiful seclu-

INTRODUCTION

sion of the Imperial gardens. The poems, it is true, generally allude to these moments, but the cares of state were many, and every day, at sunrise, officials assembled in the Audience Hall to make their reports to the Emperor. Moreover, Court ceremonials were extremely solemn occasions, carried out with the utmost dignity.

As life at Court centred about the persons of the Emperor and Empress, so life in the homes of the people centred about the elders of the family. The men of wealthy families were usually of official rank, and led a life in touch with the outer world, a life of social intercourse with other men in which friendship played an all-engrossing part. This characteristic of Chinese life is one of the most striking features of the poetic background. Love poems from men to women are so rare as to be almost non-existent (striking exceptions do occur, however, several of which are translated here), but poems of grief written at parting from "the man one loves" are innumerable, and to sit with one's friends, drinking wine and reciting verses, making music or playing chess, were favourite amusements throughout the T'ang period.

Wine-drinking was general, no pleasure gathering being complete without it. The wine of China was usually made from fermented grains, but wines from grapes, plums, pears, and other fruits were also manufactured. It was carefully heated and served in tall flagons somewhat resembling our

INTRODUCTION

coffee-pots, and was drunk out of tiny little cups no bigger than liqueur glasses. These cups, which were never of glass, were made of various metals, of lacquered or carved wood, of semi-precious stones such as jade, or agate, or carnelian; porcelain, the usual material for wine-cups today, not having yet been invented. Custom demanded that each thimbleful be tossed off at a gulp, and many were consumed before a feeling of exhilaration could be experienced. That there was a good deal of real drunkenness, we cannot doubt, but not to the extent that is generally supposed. From the character of the men and the lives they led, it is fairly clear that most of the drinking kept within reasonable bounds. Unfortunately, in translation, the quantity imbibed at these wine-parties becomes greatly exaggerated. That wine was drunk, not merely for its taste, but as a heightener of sensation, is evident; but the "three hundred cups" so often mentioned bear no such significance as might at first appear when the size of the cups is taken into account. Undoubtedly, also, we must regard this exact number as a genial hyperbole.

If husbands and sons could enjoy the excitement of travel, the spur of famous scenery, the gaieties of Court, and the pleasures of social intercourse, wives and daughters were obliged to find their occupations within the *Kuei* or "Women's Apartments," which included the gardens set apart for their use. The ruling spirit of the *Kuei* was the

INTRODUCTION

mother-in-law; and the wife of the master of the house, although she was the mother of his sons and the director of the daughters-in-law, did not reach the fulness of her power until her husband's mother had died.

The chief duty of a young wife was attendance upon her mother-in-law. With the first grey streak of daylight, she rose from her immense lacquer bed, so large as to be almost an anteroom, and, having dressed, took the old lady her tea. She then returned to her own apartment to breakfast with her husband and await the summons to attend her mother-in-law's toilet, a most solemn function, and the breakfast which followed. These duties accomplished, she was free to occupy herself as she pleased. Calligraphy, painting, writing poems and essays, were popular pursuits, and many hours were spent at the embroidery frame or in making music.

Chinese poetry is full of references to the toilet, to the intricate hair-dressing, the "moth-antennæ eyebrows," the painting of faces, and all this was done in front of a mirror standing on a little rack placed on the toilet-table. A lady, writing to her absent husband, mourns that she has no heart to "make the cloud head-dress," or writes, "looking down upon my mirror in order to apply the powder and paint, I desire to keep back the tears. I fear that the people in the house will know my grief. I am ashamed."

In spite of the fact that they had never laid eyes on the

INTRODUCTION

men they were to marry before the wedding-day, these young women seem to have depended upon the companionship of their husbands to a most touching extent. The occupations of the day were carried on in the *Kuei*; but, when evening came, the husband and wife often read and studied the classics together. A line from a well-known poem says, "The red sleeve replenishes the incense, at night, studying books," and the picture it calls up is that of a young man and woman in the typical surroundings of a Chinese home of the educated class. Red was the colour worn by very young women, whether married or not; as the years advanced, this was changed for soft blues and mauves, and later still for blacks, greys, or dull greens. A line such as "tears soak my dress of coarse, red silk" instantly suggests a young woman in deep grief.

The children studied every day with teachers; the sons and daughters of old servants who had, according to custom, taken the family surname, receiving the same advantages as those of the master. These last were, in all respects, brought up as children of the house, the only distinction being that whereas the master's own children sat "above" the table, facing South, the children of the servants sat "below," facing North. A more forcible reminder of their real status appeared later in life, since they were debarred from competing in the official examinations unless they left the household in which they had grown up and re-

INTRODUCTION

linquished the family surname taken by their fathers. A curious habit among families, which extended even to groups of friends, was the designation by numbers according to age, a man being familiarly known as Yung Seven or T'sui Fifteen. It will be noticed that such designations often occur in the poems.

Only four classes of persons were recognized as being of importance to society and these were rated in the following order: scholars, agriculturalists, labourers, and traders — officials, of course, coming under the generic name of scholars. Soldiers, actors, barbers, etc., were considered a lower order of beings entirely and, as such, properly despised.

China, essentially an agricultural country, was economically self-sufficient, producing everything needed by her population. The agriculturalist was, therefore, the very backbone of the state.

In rendering Chinese poetry, the translator must constantly keep in mind the fact that the architectural background differs from that of every other country, and that our language does not possess terms which adequately describe it.

Apart from the humble cottages of the very poor, all dwelling-houses, or *chia*, are constructed on the same general plan. They consist of a series of one-story buildings divided by courtyards, which, in the houses of the well-to-do, are connected by covered passages running along the sides of each court. A house is cut up into *chien*, or divisions, the number, within limits, being determined by the wealth and position of the owners. The homes of the people, both rich and poor, are arranged in three or five *chien*; official residences are of seven *chien*; Imperial palaces of nine. Each of these *chia* consists of several buildings, the number of which vary considerably, more buildings being added as the family grows by the marriage of the sons who, with their wives and children, are supposed to live in patriarchal fashion in their father's house. If officials sometimes carried their families with them to the towns where they were stationed, there were other posts so distant or so desolate as to make it practically impossible to take women to them. In these cases, the families remained behind under the paternal roof.

How a house was arranged can be seen in the plan at the end of this book. Doors lead to the garden from the study, the guest-room, and the Women's Apartments. These are made in an endless diversity of shapes and add greatly to the picturesqueness of house and grounds. Those through which a number of people are to pass to and fro are often large circles, while smaller and more intimate doors are cut to the outlines of fans, leaves, or flower vases. In addition to the doors, blank spaces of wall are often broken by openings at the height of a window, such openings being

INTRODUCTION

most fantastic and filled with intricately designed latticework.

I have already spoken of the *Kuei*, or Women's Apartments. In poetry, this part of the *chia* is alluded to in a highly figurative manner. The windows are "gold" or "jade" windows; the door by which it is approached is the *Lan Kuei*, or "Orchid Door." Indeed, the sweet-scented little epidendrum called by the Chinese, *lan*, is continually used to suggest the *Kuei* and its inmates.

Besides the house proper, there are numerous structures erected in gardens, for the Chinese spend much of their time in their gardens. No nation is more passionately fond of nature, whether in its grander aspects, or in the charming arrangements of potted flowers which take the place of our borders in their pleasure grounds. Among these outdoor buildings none is more difficult to describe than the *lou*, since we have nothing which exactly corresponds to it. *Lous* appear again and again in Chinese poetry, but just what to call them in English is a puzzle. They are neither summer-houses, nor pavilions, nor cupolas, but a little of all three. Always of more than one story, they are employed for differing purposes; for instance, the *fo lou* on the plan is an upper chamber where Buddhist images are kept. The *lou* generally referred to in poetry, however, is really a "pleasure-house-in-the-air," used as the Italians use their belvederes. Here the inmates of the house sit and look

INTRODUCTION

down upon the garden or over the surrounding country, or watch "the sun disappear in the long grass at the edge of the horizon" or "the moon rise like a golden hook."

Another erection foreign to Western architecture is the *t'ai*, or terrace. In early days, there were many kinds of *t'ai*, ranging from the small, square, uncovered stage still seen in private gardens and called *yüeh t'ai*, "moon terrace," to immense structures like high, long, open platforms, built by Emperors and officials for various reasons. Many of these last were famous; I have given the histories of several of them in the notes illustrating the poems, at the end of the book.

It will be observed that I have said practically nothing about religion. The reason is partly that the three principal religions practised by the Chinese are either so well known, as Buddhism, for example, or so difficult to describe, as Taoism and the ancient religion of China now merged in the teachings of Confucius; partly that none of them could be profitably compressed into the scope of this introduction; but chiefly because the subject of religion, in the poems here translated, is generally referred to in its superstitious aspects alone. The superstitions which have grown up about Taoism particularly are innumerable. I have dealt with a number of these in the notes to the poems in which they appear. Certain supernatural personages, without a

INTRODUCTION

knowledge of whom much of the poetry would be unintelligible, I have set down in the following list:

Hsien. Immortals who live in the Taoist Paradises. Human beings may attain "*Hsienship*," or Immortality, by living a life of contemplation in the hills. In translating the term, we have used the word "Immortals."

Shên. Beneficent beings who inhabit the higher regions. They are kept extremely busy attending to their duties as tutelary deities of the roads, hills, rivers, etc., and it is also their function to intervene and rescue deserving people from the attacks of their enemies.

Kuei. A proportion of the souls of the departed who inhabit the "World of Shades," a region resembling this world, which is the "World of Light," in every particular, with the important exception that it has no sunshine. Kindly *kuei* are known, but the influence generally suggested is an evil one. They may only return to the World of Light between sunset and sunrise, except upon the fifth

INTRODUCTION

                day of the Fifth Month (June), when they are free to come during the time known as the "hour of the horse," from eleven A.M. to one P.M.

Yao Kuai.   A class of fierce demons who live in the wild regions of the Southwest and delight in eating the flesh of human beings.

There are also supernatural creatures whose names carry a symbolical meaning. A few of them are:

Ch'i Lin.   A composite animal, somewhat resembling the fabulous unicorn, whose arrival is a good omen. He appears when sages are born.

Dragon.   A symbol of the forces of Heaven, also the emblem of Imperial power. Continually referred to in poetry as the steed which transports a philosopher who has attained Immortality to his home in the Western Paradise.

Fêng Huang.   A glorious bird, symbol of the Empress, therefore often associated with the dragon. The conception of this bird is probably based on the Argus pheasant. It is described as possessing every grace

INTRODUCTION

and beauty. A Chinese author, quoted by F. W. Williams in "The Middle Kingdom," writes: "It resembles a wild swan before and a unicorn behind; it has the throat of a swallow, the bill of a cock, the neck of a snake, the tail of a fish, the forehead of a crane, the crown of a mandarin drake, the stripes of a dragon, and the vaulted back of a tortoise. The feathers have five colours which are named after the five cardinal virtues, and it is five cubits in height; the tail is graduated like the pipes of a gourd-organ, and its song resembles the music of the instrument, having five modulations." Properly speaking, the female is *Fêng*, the male *Huang*, but the two words are usually given in combination to denote the species. Some one, probably in desperation, once translated the combined words as "phœnix," and this term has been employed ever since. It conveys, however, an entirely wrong impression of the creature. To Western readers, the word "phœnix" suggests a bird which, being consumed by fire,

INTRODUCTION

rises in a new birth from its own ashes. The *Fêng Huang* has no such power, it is no symbol of hope or resurrection, but suggests friendship and affection of all sorts. Miss Lowell and I have translated the name as "crested love-pheasant," which seems to us to convey a better idea of the beautiful *Fêng Huang*, the bird which brings happiness.

Luan. A supernatural bird sometimes confused with the above. It is a sacred creature, connected with fire, and a symbol of love and passion, of the relation between men and women.

Chien. The "paired-wings bird," described in Chinese books as having but one wing and one eye, for which reason two must unite for either of them to fly. It is often referred to as suggesting undying affection.

Real birds and animals also have symbolical attributes. I give only three:

Crane. Represents longevity, and is employed, as is the dragon, to transport those who

INTRODUCTION

have attained to Immortality to the Heavens.

Yuan Yang.
: The exquisite little mandarin ducks, an unvarying symbol of conjugal fidelity. Li T'ai-po often alludes to them and declares that, rather than be separated, they would "prefer to die ten thousand deaths, and have their gauze-like wings torn to fragments."

Wild Geese.
: Symbols of direct purpose, their flight being always in a straight line. As they follow the sun's course, allusions to their departure suggest Spring, to their arrival, Autumn.

A complete list of the trees and plants endowed with symbolical meanings would be almost endless. Those most commonly employed in poetry in a suggestive sense are:

Ch'ang P'u.
: A plant growing in the Taoist Paradise and much admired by the Immortals, who are the only beings able to see its purple blossoms. On earth, it is known as the sweet flag, and has the peculiarity of never blossoming. It is hung on the lintels of doors on the fifth day of the

INTRODUCTION

	Fifth Month to ward off the evil influences which may be brought by the *kuei* on their return to this world during the "hour of the horse."
Peony.	Riches and prosperity.
Lotus.	Purity. Although it rises from the mud, it is bright and spotless.
Plum-blossom.	Literally "the first," it being the first of the "hundred flowers" to open. It suggests the beginnings of things, and is also one of the "three friends" who do not fear the Winter cold, the other two being the pine and the bamboo.
Lan.	A small epidendrum, translated in this book as "spear-orchid." It is a symbol for noble men and beautiful, refined women. Confucius compared the *Chün Tzŭ*, Princely or Superior Man, to this little orchid with its delightful scent. In poetry, it is also used in reference to the Women's Apartments and everything connected with them, suggesting, as it does, the extreme of refinement.
Chrysanthemum.	Fidelity and constancy. Inspite of frost, its flowers continue to bloom.

INTRODUCTION

Ling Chih.	Longevity. This fungus, which grows at the roots of trees, is very durable when dried.
Pine.	Longevity, immutability, steadfastness.
Bamboo.	This plant has as many virtues as it has uses, the principal ones are modesty, protection from defilement, unchangeableness.
Wu-t'ung.	A tree whose botanical name is *sterculia platanifolia*. Its only English name seems to be "umbrella-tree," which has proved so unattractive in its context in the poems that we have left it untranslated. It is a symbol for integrity, high principles, great sensibility. When "Autumn stands," on August seventh, although it is still to all intents and purposes Summer, the wu-t'ung tree drops one leaf. Its wood, which is white, easy to cut, and very light, is the only kind suitable for making that intimate instrument which quickly betrays the least emotion of the person playing upon it — the *ch'in*, or table-lute.

INTRODUCTION

Willow.
A prostitute, or any very frivolous person. Concubines writing to their lords often refer to themselves under this figure, in the same spirit of self-depreciation which prompts them to employ the euphemism, "Unworthy One," instead of the personal pronoun. Because of its lightness and pliability, it conveys also the idea of extreme vitality.

Peach-blossom.
Beautiful women and ill-success in life. The first suggestion, on account of the exquisite colour of the flower; the second, because of its perishability.

Peach-tree.
Longevity. This fruit is supposed to ripen once every three thousand years on the trees of Paradise, and those who eat of this celestial species never die.

Mulberry.
Utility. Also suggests a peaceful hamlet. Its wood is used in the making of bows and the kind of temple-drums called *mo yü* — wooden fish. Its leaves feed the silk-worms.

Plantain.
Sadness and grief. It is symbolical of a heart which is not "flat" or "level," as

INTRODUCTION

the Chinese say, not open or care-free, but of one which is "tightly rolled." The sound of rain on its leaves is very mournful, therefore an allusion to the plantain always means sorrow. Planted outside windows already glazed with silk, its heavy green leaves soften the glaring light of Summer, and it is often used for this purpose.

Nothing has been more of a stumbling-block to translators than the fact that the Chinese year — which is strictly lunar, with an intercalary month added at certain intervals — begins a month later than ours; or, to be more exact, it is calculated from the first new moon after the sun enters Aquarius, which brings the New Year at varying times from the end of January to the middle of February. For translation purposes, however, it is safe to count the Chinese months as always one later by our calendar than the number given would seem to imply. By this calculation the "First Month" is February, and so on throughout the year.

The day is divided into twelve periods of two hours each beginning at eleven P.M. and each of these periods is called by the name of an animal — horse, deer, snake, bat, etc. As these names are not duplicated, the use of them tells at

INTRODUCTION

once whether the hour is day or night. Ancient China's method of telling time was by means of slow and evenly burning sticks made of a composition of clay and sawdust, or by the clepsydra, or water-clock. Water-clocks are mentioned several times in these poems.

So much for what I have called the backgrounds of Chinese poetry. I must now speak of that poetry itself, and of Miss Lowell's and my method of translating it.

Chinese prosody is a very difficult thing for an Occidental to understand. Chinese is a monosyllabic language, and this reduces the word-sounds so considerably that speech would be almost impossible were it not for the invention of tones by which the same sound can be made to do the duty of four in the Mandarin dialect, five in the Nankingese, nine in the Cantonese, etc., a different tone inflection totally changing the meaning of a word. Only two chief tones are used in poetry, the "level" and the "oblique," but the oblique tone is subdivided into three, which makes four different inflections possible to every sound. Of course, like English and other languages, the same word may have several meanings, and in Chinese these meanings are bewilderingly many; the only possible way of determining which one is correct is by its context. These tones constitute, at the outset, the principal difference which divides the technique of Chinese poetry from our own. Another is to be found in the fact that nothing approaching our metri-

INTRODUCTION

cal foot is possible in a tongue which knows only single syllables. Rhyme does exist, but there are only a little over a hundred rhymes, as tone inflection does not change a word in that particular. Such a paucity of rhyme would seriously affect the richness of any poetry, if again the Chinese had not overcome this lingual defect by the employment of a juxtaposing pattern made up of their four poetic tones. And these tones come to the rescue once more when we consider the question of rhythm. Monosyllables in themselves always produce a staccato effect, which tends to make all rhythm composed of them monotonous, if, indeed, it does not destroy it altogether. The tones cause what I may call a psychological change in the time-length of these monosyllables, which change not only makes true rhythm possible, but allows marked varieties of the basic beat.

One of the chief differences between poetry and prose is that poetry must have a more evident pattern. The pattern of Chinese poetry is formed out of three elements: line, rhyme, and tone.

The Chinese attitude toward line is almost identical with that of the French. French prosody counts every syllable as a foot, and a line is made up of so many counted feet. If any of my readers has ever read French alexandrines aloud to a Frenchman, read them as we should read English poetry, seeking to bring out the musical stress, he will remember the look of sad surprise which crept over his

INTRODUCTION

hearer's face. Not so was this verse constructed; not so is it to be read. The number of syllables to a line is counted, that is the secret of French classic poetry; the number of syllables is counted in Chinese. But — and we come to a divergence — this method of counting does, in French practice, often do away with the rhythm so delightful to an English ear; in Chinese, no such violence occurs, as each syllable is a word and no collection of such words can fall into a metric pulse as French words can, and, in their *Chansons*, are permitted to do.

The Chinese line pattern is, then, one of counted words, and these counted words are never less than three, nor more than seven, in regular verse; irregular is a different matter, as I shall explain shortly. Five and seven word lines are cut by a cæsura, which comes after the second word in a five-word line, and after the fourth in a seven-word line.

Rhyme is used exactly as we use it, at the ends of lines. Internal rhyming is common, however, in a type of poem called a "*fu*," which I shall deal with when I come to the particular kinds of verse.

Tone is everywhere, obviously, and is employed, not arbitrarily, but woven into a pattern of its own which again is in a more or less loose relation to rhyme. By itself, the tone-pattern alternates in a peculiar manner in each line, the last line of a stanza conforming to the order of tones in the first, the intervening lines varying methodi-

INTRODUCTION

cally. I have before me a poem in which the tone-pattern is alike in lines one, four, and eight, of an eight-line stanza, as are lines two and six, and lines three and seven, while line five is the exact opposite of lines two and six. In the second stanza of the same poem, the pattern is kept, but adversely; the tones do not follow the same order, but conform in similarity of grouping. I use this example merely to show what is meant by tone-pattern. It will serve to illustrate how much diversity and richness this tone-chiming is capable of bringing to Chinese poetry.

Words which rhyme must be in the same tone in regular verse, and unrhymed lines must end on an oblique tone if the rhyme-tone is level, and *vice versa*. The level tone is preferred for rhyme.

In the early Chinese poetry, called *Ku-shih* (Old Poems), the tones were practically disregarded. But in the *Lü-shih* (Regulated Poems) the rules regarding them are very strict. The *lü-shih* are supposed to date from the beginning of the T'ang Dynasty. A *lü-shih* poem proper should be of eight lines, though this is often extended to sixteen, but it must be in either the five-word line, or the seven-word line, metre. The poets of the T'ang Dynasty, however, were by no means the slaves of *lü-shih*; they went their own way, as good poets always do, conforming when it pleased them and disregarding when they chose. It depended on the character of the poet. Tu Fu was renowned for his careful

INTRODUCTION

versification; Li T'ai-po, on the other hand, not infrequently rebelled and made his own rules. In his "Drinking Song," which is in seven-word lines, he suddenly dashes in two three-word lines, a proceeding which must have been greatly upsetting to the purists. It is amusing to note that his "Taking Leave of Tu Fu" is in the strictest possible form, which is at once a tribute and a poking of fun at his great friend and contemporary.

Regular poems of more than sixteen lines are called *p'ai lu*, and these may run to any length; Tu Fu carried them to forty, eighty, and even to two hundred lines. Another form, always translated as "short-stop," cuts the eight-line poem in two. In theory, the short-stop holds the same relation to the eight-line poem that the Japanese *hokku* does to the *tanka*, although of course it preceded the *hokku* by many centuries. It is supposed to suggest rather than to state, being considered as an eight-line poem with its end in the air. In suggestion, however, the later Japanese form far outdoes it.

So called "irregular verse" follows the writer's inclination within the natural limits of all Chinese prosody.

A *tzŭ* may be taken to mean a lyric, if we use that term, not in its dictionary sense, but as all modern poets employ it. It may vary its line length, but must keep the same variation in all the stanzas.

Perhaps the most interesting form to modern students is

INTRODUCTION

the *fu*, in which the construction is almost identical with that of "polyphonic prose." The lines are so irregular in length that the poem might be mistaken for prose, had we not a corresponding form to guide us. The rhymes appear when and where they will, in the middle of the lines or at the end, and sometimes there are two or more together. I have been told that Persia has, or had, an analogous form, and if so modern an invention as "polyphonic prose" derives, however unconsciously, from two such ancient countries as China and Persia, the fact is, at least, interesting.

The earliest examples of Chinese poetry which have come down to us are a collection of rhymed ballads in various metres, of which the most usual is four words to a line. They are simple, straightforward pieces, often of a strange poignance, and always reflecting the quiet, peaceful habits of a people engaged in agriculture. The oldest were probably composed about 2000 B.C. and the others at varying times from then until the Sixth Century B.C., when Confucius gathered them into the volume known as the "Book of Odes." Two of these odes are translated in this book. The next epoch in the advance of poetry-making was introduced by Ch'ü Yüan (312-295 B.C.), a famous statesman and poet, who wrote an excitable, irregular style in which the primitive technical rules were disregarded, their place being taken by exigencies of emotion and idea. We are wont to regard a poetical technique determined by

INTRODUCTION

feeling alone as a very modern innovation, and it is interesting to note that the method is, on the contrary, as old as the hills. These rhapsodical allegories culminated in a poem entitled "Li Sao," or "Falling into Trouble," which is one of the most famous of ancient Chinese poems. A further development took place under the Western Han (206 B.C.–A.D. 25), when Su Wu invented the five-character poem, *ku fêng*; these poems were in Old Style, but had five words to a line. It is during this same period that poems with seven words to a line appeared. Legend has it that they were first composed by the Emperor Wu of Han, and that he hit upon the form on an occasion when he and his Ministers were drinking wine and capping verses at a feast on the White Beam Terrace. Finally, under the Empress Wu Hou, early in the T'ang Dynasty, the *lü-shih*, or "poems according to law," became the standard. It will be seen that the *lü-shih* found the five and seven word lines already in being and had merely to standardize them. The important gift which the *lü-shih* brought to Chinese prosody was its insistence on tone.

The great period of Chinese poetry was during the T'ang Dynasty. Then lived the three famous poets, Li T'ai-po, Tu Fu, and Po Chü-i. Space forbids me to give the biographies of all the poets whose work is included in this volume, but as Li T'ai-po and Tu Fu, between them, take up more than half the book, a short account of the princi-

INTRODUCTION

pal events of their lives seems necessary. I shall take them in the order of the number of their poems printed in this collection, which also, as a matter of fact, happens to be chronological.

I have already stated in the first part of this Introduction the reasons which determined me to give so large a space to Li T'ai-po. English writers on Chinese literature are fond of announcing that Li T'ai-po is China's greatest poet; the Chinese themselves, however, award this place to Tu Fu. We may put it that Li T'ai-po was the people's poet, and Tu Fu the poet of scholars. As Po Chü-i is represented here by only one poem, no account of his life has been given. A short biography of him may be found in Mr. Waley's "A Hundred and Seventy Chinese Poems."

It is permitted to very few to live in the hearts of their countrymen as Li T'ai-po has lived in the hearts of the Chinese. To-day, twelve hundred and twenty years after his birth, his memory and his fame are fresh, his poems are universally recited, his personality is familiar on the stage: in fact, to use the words of a Chinese scholar, "It may be said that there is no one in the People's Country who does not know the name of Li T'ai-po." Many legends are told of his birth, his life, his death, and he is now numbered among the *Hsien* (Immortals) who inhabit the Western Paradise.

Li T'ai-po was born A.D. 701, of well-to-do parents named Li, who lived in the Village of the Green Lotus in Szechwan.

INTRODUCTION

He is reported to have been far more brilliant than ordinary children. When he was only five years old, he read books that other boys read at ten; at ten, he could recite the "Classics" aloud and had read the "Book of the Hundred Sages." Doubtless this precocity was due to the fact that his birth was presided over by the "Metal Star," which we know as Venus. His mother dreamt that she had conceived him under the influence of this luminary, and called him T'ai-po, "Great Whiteness," a popular name for the planet.

In spite of his learning, he was no *Shu Tai Tzǔ* (Book Idiot) as the Chinese say, but, on the contrary, grew up a strong young fellow, impetuous to a fault, with a lively, enthusiastic nature. He was extremely fond of sword-play, and constantly made use of his skill in it to right the wrongs of his friends. However worthy his causes may have been, this propensity got him into a serious scrape. In the excitement of one of these encounters, he killed several people, and was forthwith obliged to fly from his native village. The situation was an awkward one, but the young man disguised himself as a servant and entered the employ of a minor official. This gentleman was possessed of literary ambitions and a somewhat halting talent; still we can hardly wonder that he was not pleased when his servant ended a poem in which he was hopelessly floundering with lines far better than he could make. After this, and one or two similar experiences, Li T'ai-po found it advisa-

INTRODUCTION

ble to relinquish his job and depart from his master's house.

His next step was to join a scholar who disguised his real name under the pseudonym of "Stern Son of the East." The couple travelled together to the beautiful Min Mountains, where they lived in retirement for five years as teacher and pupil. This period, passed in reading, writing, discussing literature, and soaking in the really marvellous scenery, greatly influenced the poet's future life, and imbued him with that passionate love for nature so apparent in his work.

At the age of twenty-five, he separated from his teacher and left the mountains, going home to his native village for a time. But the love of travel was inherent in him, nowhere could hold him for long, and he soon started off on a sight-seeing trip to all those places in the Empire famous for their beauty. This time he travelled as the position of his parents warranted, and even a little beyond it. He had a retinue of servants, and spent money lavishly. This open-handedness is one of the fine traits of his character. Needy scholars and men of talent never appealed to him in vain; during a year at Yangchow, he is reported to have spent three hundred thousand ounces of silver in charity.

From Yangchow he journeyed to the province of Hupeh ("North of the Lake") where, in the district of the "Dreary Clouds," he stayed at the house of a family named

INTRODUCTION

Hsü, which visit resulted in his marriage with one of the daughters. Li T'ai-po lived in Hupeh for some years — he himself says three — then his hunger for travel reasserted itself and he was off again. After some years of wandering, while visiting a magistrate in Shantung, an incident occurred which had far-reaching consequences. A prisoner was about to be flogged. Li T'ai-po, who was passing, glanced at the man, and, happening to be possessed of a shrewd insight into character, realized at once that here was an unusual person. He secured the man's release, and twenty-five years later this action bore fruit as the sequel will show. The freed prisoner was Kuo Tzŭ-i, who became one of China's most powerful generals and the saviour of the T'ang Dynasty.

It will be noticed that nothing has been said of the poet taking any examinations, and for the excellent reason that he never thought it worth while to present himself as a candidate. The simple fact appears to be that geniuses often do not seem to find necessary what other men consider of supreme importance. Presumably, also, he had no particular desire for an official life. The gifts of Heaven go by favour and the gifts of man are strangely apt to do the same thing, in spite of the excellent rules devised to order them. Li T'ai-po's career owed nothing to either the lack of official degrees or official interest. What he achieved, he owed to himself; what he failed in came from the same source.

INTRODUCTION

About this time, the poet and a few congenial friends formed the coterie of "The Six Idlers of the Bamboo Brook." They retired to the Ch'u Lai Mountain and spent their time in drinking, reciting poems, writing beautiful characters, and playing on the table-lute. It must be admitted that Li T'ai-po was an inveterate and inordinate drinker, and far more often than was wise in the state called by his countrymen "great drunk." To this propensity he was indebted for all his ill fortune, as it was to his poetic genius that he owed all his good.

So the years passed until, when he was forty-two, he met the Taoist priest, Wu Yün. They immediately became intimate, and on Wu Yün's being called to the capital, Li T'ai-po accompanied him. Wu Yün took occasion to tell the Emperor of his friend's extraordinary talent. The Emperor was interested, the poet was sent for, and, introduced by Ho Chih-chang, was received by the Son of Heaven in the Golden Bells Hall.

The native accounts of this meeting state that "in his discourses upon the affairs of the Empire, the words rushed from his mouth like a mountain torrent." Ming Huang, who was enchanted, ordered food to be brought and helped the poet himself.

So Li T'ai-po became attached to the Court and was made an honorary member of the "Forest of Pencils." He was practically the Emperor's secretary and wrote the

INTRODUCTION

Emperor's edicts, but this was by the way — his real duty was simply to write what he chose and when, and recite these poems at any moment that it pleased the Emperor to call upon him to do so.

Li T'ai-po, with his love of wine and good-fellowship, was well suited for the life of the gay and dissipated Court of Ming Huang, then completely under the influence of the beautiful concubine, Yang Kuei-fei. Conspicuous among the Emperor's entourage was Ho Chih-chang, a famous statesman, poet, and calligraphist, who, on reading Li T'ai-po's poetry, is said to have sighed deeply and exclaimed: "This is not the work of a human being, but of a *Tsê Hsien* (Banished Immortal)." To understand fully the significance of this epithet, it must be realized that mortals who have already attained Immortality, but who have committed some fault, may be banished from Paradise to expiate their sin on earth.

For about two years, Li T'ai-po led the life of supreme favourite in the most brilliant Court in the world. The fact that when sent for to compose or recite verses he was not unapt to be drunk was of no particular importance since, after being summarily revived with a dash of cold water, he could always write or chant with his accustomed verve and dexterity. His influence over the Emperor became so great that it roused the jealousy, and eventually the hatred, of Kao Li-shih, the Chief Eunuch, who, until

INTRODUCTION

then, had virtually ruled his Imperial master. On one occasion, when Li T'ai-po was more than usually incapacitated, the Emperor ordered Kao to take off the poet's shoes. This was too much, and from that moment the eunuch's malignity became an active intriguing to bring about his rival's downfall. He found the opportunity he needed in the vanity of Yang Kuei-fei. Persuading this lady that Li T'ai-po's "Songs to the Peonies" contained a veiled insult directed at her, he enlisted her anger against the poet and so gained an important ally to his cause. On three separate occasions when Ming Huang wished to confer official rank upon the poet, Yang Kuei-fei interfered and persuaded the Emperor to forego his intention. Li T'ai-po was of too independent a character, and too little of a courtier, to lift a finger to placate his enemies. But the situation became so acute that at last he begged leave to retire from the Court altogether. His request granted, he immediately formed a new group of seven congenial souls and with them departed once more to the mountains. This new association called itself "The Eight Immortals of the Wine-cup."

Although Li T'ai-po had asked for his own dismissal, he had really been forced to ask it, and his banishment from the "Imperial Sun," with all that "Sun" implied, was a blow from which he never recovered. His later poems are full of more or less veiled allusions to his unhappy state.

INTRODUCTION

The next ten years were spent in his favourite occupation of travelling, especially in the provinces of Szechwan, Hunan, and Hupeh.

Meanwhile, political conditions were growing steadily worse. Popular discontent at the excesses of Yang Kueifei and her satellite An Lu-shan were increasing, and finally, in A.D. 755, rebellion broke out. I have dealt with this rebellion earlier in this Introduction, and a more detailed account is given in the Notes; I shall, therefore, do no more than mention it here. Sometime during the preceding unrest, Li T'ai-po, weary of moving from place to place, had taken the position of adviser to Li Ling, Prince of Yung. In the wide-spread disorder caused by the rebellion, Li Ling conceived the bold idea of establishing himself South of the Yangtze as Emperor on his own account. Pursuing his purpose, he started at the head of his troops for Nanking. Li T'ai-po strongly disapproved of the Prince's course, a disapproval which affected that headstrong person not at all, and the poet was forced to accompany his master on the march to Nanking.

At Nanking, the Prince's army was defeated by the Imperial troops, and immediately after the disaster Li T'ai-po fled, but was caught, imprisoned, and condemned to death. Now came the sequel to the incident which had taken place long before at Shantung. The Commander of the Imperial forces was no other than Kuo Tzŭ-i, the

INTRODUCTION

former prisoner whose life Li T'ai-po had saved. On learning the sentence passed upon the poet, Kuo Tzŭ-i intervened and threatened to resign his command unless his benefactor were spared. Accordingly Li T'ai-po's sentence was changed to exile and he was released, charged to depart immediately for some great distance where he could do no harm. He set out for Yeh Lang, a desolate spot beyond the "Five Streams," in Kueichow. This was the country of the *yao kuai*, the man-eating demons; and whether he believed in them or not, the thought of existence in such a gloomy solitude must have filled him with desperation.

He had not gone far, luckily, when a general amnesty was declared, and he was permitted to return and live with his friend and disciple, Lu Yang-ping, in the Lu Mountains near Kiukiang, a place which he dearly loved. Here, in A.D. 762, at the age of sixty-one, he died, bequeathing all his manuscripts to Lu Yang-ping.

The tale of his drowning, repeated by Giles and others, is pure legend, as an authoritative statement of Lu Yang-ping proves. The manuscripts left to his care, and all others he could collect from friends, Lu Yang-ping published in an edition of ten volumes. This edition appeared in the year of the poet's death, and contained the following preface by Lu Yang-ping:

> Since the three dynasties of antiquity,
> Since the style of the 'Kuo Fêng' and the 'Li Sao,'

INTRODUCTION

> During these thousand years and more, of those who walked the "lonely path,"
> There has been only you, you are the Solitary Man, you are without rival.

Li T'ai-po's poetry is full of dash and surprise. At his best, there is an extraordinary exhilaration in his work; at his worst, he is merely repetitive. Chinese critics have complained that his subjects are all too apt to be trivial, and that his range is narrow. This is quite true; poems of farewell, deserted ladies sighing for their absent lords, officials consumed by homesickness, pæans of praise for wine — in the aggregate there are too many of these. But how fine they often are! "The Lonely Wife," "Poignant Grief During a Sunny Spring," "After being Separated for a Long Time," such poems are the truth of emotion. Take again his inimitable humour in the two "Drinking Alone in the Moonlight" poems, or "Statement of Resolutions after being Drunk on a Spring Day." Then there are the poems of hyperbolical description such as "The Perils of the Shu Road," "The Northern Flight," and "The Terraced Road of the Two-Edged Sword Mountains." Mountains seem to be in his very blood. Of the sea, on the other hand, he has no such intimate knowledge; he sees it afar, from some height, but always as a thing apart, a distant view. The sea he gazes at; the mountains he treads under foot, their creepers scratch his face, the jutting rocks beside the path bruise his hands. He knows the

INTRODUCTION

straight-up, cutting-into-the-sky look of mountain peaks just above him, and feels, almost bodily, the sheer drop into the angry river tearing its way through a narrow gully below, a river he can see only by leaning dangerously far over the cliff upon which he is standing. There is a curious sense of perpendicularity about these mountain rhapsodies. The vision is strained up for miles, and shot suddenly down for hundreds of feet. The tactile effect of them is astounding; they are not to be read, but experienced. And yet I am loth to say that Li T'ai-po is at his greatest in description, with poems so full of human passion and longing as "The Lonely Wife," and "Poignant Grief During a Sunny Spring," before me. There is no doubt at all that in Li T'ai-po we have one of the world's greatest lyrics.

Great though he was, it cannot be denied that he had serious weaknesses. One was his tendency to write when the mood was not there, and at these moments he was not ashamed to repeat a fancy conceived before on some other occasion. Much of his style he crystallized into a convention, and brought it out unblushingly whenever he was at a loss for something to say. Sustained effort evidently wearied him. He will begin a poem with the utmost spirit, but his energy is apt to flag and lead to a close so weak as to annoy the reader. His short poems are always admirably built, the endings complete and unexpected; the architectonics of his long poems leave much to be desired. He seems

INTRODUCTION

to be ridden by his own emotion, but without the power to draw it up and up to a climax; it bursts upon us in the first line, sustains itself at the same level for a series of lines, and then seems to faint exhausted, reducing the poet to the necessity of stopping as quickly as he can and with as little jar as possible. Illustrations of this tendency to a weak ending can be seen in "The Lonely Wife," "The Perils of the Shu Road," and "The Terraced Road of the Two-Edged Sword Mountains," but that he could keep his inspiration to the end on occasion, "The Northern Flight" proves.

Finally, there are his poems of battle: "Songs of the Marches," "Battle to the South of the City," and "Fighting to the South of the City." Nothing can be said of these except that they are superb. If there is a hint of let-down in the concluding lines of "Fighting to the South of the City," it is due to the frantic Chinese desire to quote from older authors, and this is an excellent example of the chief vice of Chinese poetry, since these two lines are taken from the "Tao Tê Ching," the sacred book of Taoism; the others, even the long "Songs of the Marches," are admirably sustained.

In Mr. Waley's excellent monograph on Li T'ai-po, appears the following paragraph: "Wang An-shih (A.D. 1021–1086), the great reformer of the Eleventh Century, observes: 'Li Po's style is swift, yet never careless; lively, yet

INTRODUCTION

never informal. But his intellectual outlook was low and sordid. In nine poems out of ten he deals with nothing but wine and women.'" A somewhat splenetic criticism truly, but great reformers have seldom either the acumen or the sympathy necessary for the judgment of poetry. Women and wine there are in abundance, but how treated? In no mean or sordid manner certainly. Li T'ai-po was not a didactic poet, and we of the Twentieth Century may well thank fortune for that. Peradventure the Twenty-first will dote again upon the didactic, but we must follow our particular inclination which is, it must be admitted, quite counter to anything of the sort. No low or mean attitude indeed, but a rather restricted one we may, if we please, charge against Li T'ai-po. He was a sensuous realist, representing the world as he saw it, with beauty as his guiding star. Conditions to him were static; he wasted none of his force in speculating on what they should be. A scene or an emotion *was*, and it was his business to reproduce it, not to analyze how it had come about or what would best make its recurrence impossible. Here he is at sharp variance with Tu Fu, who probes to the roots of events even when he appears to be merely describing them. One has but to compare the "Songs of the Marches" and "Battle to the South of the City" with "The Recruiting Officers" and "Crossing the Frontier" to see the difference.

Tu Fu was born in Tu Ling, in the province of Shensi,

INTRODUCTION

in A.D. 713. His family was extremely poor, but his talent was so marked that at seven years old he had begun to write poetry; at nine, he could write large characters; and at fifteen, his essays and poems were the admiration of his small circle. When he was twenty-four, he went up to Ch'ang An, the capital, for his first examination — it will be remembered that, in the T'ang period, all the examinations took place at Ch'ang An. Tu Fu was perfectly qualified to pass, as every one was very well aware, but the opinions he expressed in his examination papers were so radical that the degree was withheld. There was nothing to be done, and Tu Fu took to wandering about the country, observing and writing, but with little hope of anything save poverty to come. On one of his journeys, he met Li T'ai-po on the "Lute Terrace" in Ching Hsien. The two poets, who sincerely admired each other, became the closest friends. Several poems in this collection are addressed by one to the other.

When Tu Fu was thirty-six, it happened that the Emperor sent out invitations to all the scholars in the Empire to come to the capital and compete in an examination. Tu Fu was, of course, known to the Emperor as a man who would have been promoted but for the opinions aired in his papers. Of his learning, there could be no shadow of doubt. So Tu Fu went to Ch'ang An and waited there as an "expectant official." He waited for four years, when it oc-

INTRODUCTION

curred to him to offer three *fu* to the Emperor. The event justified his temerity, and the poet was given a post as one of the officials in the Chih Hsien library. This post he held for four years, when he was appointed to a slightly better one at Fêng-hsien. But, a year later, the An Lu-shan rebellion broke out, which put a summary end to Tu Fu's position, whereupon he left Fêng-hsien and went to live with a relative at the Village of White Waters. He was still living there when the Emperor Ming Huang abdicated in favour of his son, Su Tsung. If the old Emperor had given him an office, perhaps the new one would; at any rate it was worth an attempt, for Tu Fu was in dire poverty. Having no money to hire any kind of conveyance, he started to walk to his destination, but fell in with brigands who captured him. He stayed with these brigands for over a year, but finally escaped, and at length reached Fêng Chiang, where the Emperor was in residence.

His appearance on his arrival was miserable in the extreme. Haggard and thin, his shoulders sticking out of his coat, his rags literally tied together, he was indeed a spectacle to inspire pity, and the Emperor at once appointed him to the post of Censor. But this did not last long. He had the imprudence to remonstrate with the Emperor anent the sentence of banishment passed upon the general Tan Kuan. Considering that this clever and extremely learned soldier had so far relaxed the discipline of his army

INTRODUCTION

during one of the Northern campaigns that, one night, when his troops were all peacefully sleeping in their chariots, the camp was surrounded and burnt and his forces utterly routed, the punishment seems deserved. But Tu Fu thought otherwise, and so unwisely urged his opinion that the Emperor lost patience and ordered an investigation of Tu Fu's conduct. His friends, however, rallied to his defence and the investigation was quashed, but he was deprived of the censorship and sent to a minor position in Shensi. This he chose to regard as a punishment, as indeed it was. He proceeded to Shensi, but, on arriving there, dramatically refused to assume his office; having performed which act of bravado, he joined his family in Kansu. He found them in the greatest distress from famine, and although he did his best to keep them alive by going to the hills and gathering fire-wood to sell, and by digging up roots and various growing things for them to eat, several of his children died of starvation.

Another six months of minor officialdom in Hua Chou, and he retired to Ch'êngtu in Szechwan, where he lived in a grass-roofed house, engaged in study and the endeavour to make the two ends of nothing meet. At length, a friend of his arrived in Szechwan as Governor-General, and this friend appointed him a State Counsellor. But the grass-house was more to his taste than state councils, and after a year and a half he returned to

INTRODUCTION

it, and the multifarious wanderings which always punctuated his life.

Five years later, when he was fifty-five, he set off on one of his journeys, but was caught by floods and obliged to take refuge in a ruined temple at Hu Kuang, where he nearly starved before help could reach him. After ten days, he was rescued through the efforts of the local magistrate, but eating again after so long a fast was fatal and he died within an hour.

Innumerable essays have been written comparing the styles of Li T'ai-po and Tu Fu. Yüan Chên, a poet of the T'ang period, says that Tu Fu's poems have perfect balance; that, if he wrote a thousand lines, the last would have as much vigour as the first and that no one can equal him in this, his poems make a "perfect circle." He goes on: "In my opinion, the great living wave of poetry and song in which Li T'ai-po excelled is surpassed in Tu Fu's work, he is shoulder higher than Li Po." Again: "The poems of Li T'ai-po are like Spring flowers, those of Tu Fu are like the pine-trees, they are eternal and fear neither snow nor cold."

Shên Ming-chên says: "Li Po is like the Spring grass, like Autumn waves, not a person but must love him. Tu Fu is like a great hill, a high peak, a long river, the broad sea, like fine grass and bright-coloured flowers, like a pine or an ancient fir, like moving wind and gentle waves, like

INTRODUCTION

heavy hoar-frost, like burning heat — not a quality is missing."

Hu Yu-ling uses a metaphor referring to casting dice and says that Li T'ai-po would owe Tu Fu "an ivory"; and Han Yü, speaking of both Li T'ai-po and Tu Fu, declares that "the flaming light of their essays would rise ten thousand feet."

Poetic as these criticisms are, it is their penetration which is so astonishing; but I think the most striking comparison made of Tu Fu's work is that by Tao Kai-yu: "Tu Fu's poems are like pictures, like the branches of trees reflected in water — the branches of still trees. Like a large group of houses seen through clouds or mist, they appear and disappear."

Sometime ago, in a review of a volume of translations of Chinese poetry in the London "Times," I came across this remarkable statement: "The Chinese poet starts talking in the most ordinary language and voices the most ordinary things, and his poetry seems to happen suddenly out of the commonplace as if it were some beautiful action happening in the routine of actual life."

The critic could have had no knowledge of the Chinese language, as nothing can be farther from the truth than his observation. It is largely a fact that the Oriental poet finds his themes in the ordinary affairs of everyday life, but he describes them in a very special, carefully chosen,

INTRODUCTION

medium. The simplest child's primer is written in a language never used in speaking, while the most highly educated scholar would never dream of employing the same phrases in conversation which he would make use of were he writing an essay, a poem, or a state document. Each language — the spoken, the poetic, the literary, the documentary — has its own construction, its own class of characters, and its own symbolism. A translator must therefore make a special study of whichever he wishes to render.

Although several great sinologues have written on the subject of Chinese poetry, none, so far as I am aware, has devoted his exclusive attention to the poetic style, nor has any translator availed himself of the assistance, so essential to success, of a poet — that is, one trained in the art of seizing the poetic values in fine shades of meaning. Without this power, which amounts to an instinct, no one can hope to reproduce any poetry in another tongue, and how much truer this is of Chinese poetry can only be realized by those who have some knowledge of the language. Such poets, on the other hand, as have been moved to make beautiful renditions of Chinese originals have been hampered by inadequate translations. It is impossible to expect that even a scholar thoroughly versed in the philological aspects of Chinese literature can, at the same time, be endowed with enough of the poetic *flair* to convey, uninjured, the thoughts

INTRODUCTION

of one poet to another. A second personality obtrudes between poet and poet, and the contact, which must be established between the two minds if any adequate translation is to result, is broken. How Miss Lowell and I have endeavoured to obviate this rupture of the poetic current, I shall explain presently. But, to understand it, another factor in the case must first be understood.

It cannot be too firmly insisted upon that the Chinese character itself plays a considerable part in Chinese poetic composition. Calligraphy and poetry are mixed up together in the Chinese mind. How close this intermingling may be, will appear when we come to speak of the "Written Pictures," but even without following the interdependence of these arts to the point where they merge into one, it must not be forgotten that Chinese is an ideographic, or picture, language. These marvellous collections of brush-strokes which we call Chinese characters are really separate pictographic representations of complete thoughts. Complex characters are not spontaneously composed, but are built up of simple characters, each having its own peculiar meaning and usage; these, when used in combination, each play their part in modifying either the sense or the sound of the complex. Now it must not be thought that these separate entities make an over-loud noise in the harmony of the whole character. They are each subdued to the total result, the final meaning, but they do produce a qualifying

INTRODUCTION

effect upon the word itself. Since Chinese characters are complete ideas, it is convenient to be able to express the various degrees of these ideas by special characters which shall have those exact meanings; it is, therefore, clear that to grasp a poet's full intention in a poem there must be a knowledge of the analysis of characters.

This might seem bizarre, were it not for a striking proof to the contrary. It is a fact that many of the Chinese characters have become greatly altered during the centuries since they were invented. So long ago as A.D. 200, a scholar named Hsü Shih, realizing that this alteration was taking place, wrote the dictionary known as "Shuo Wên Chieh Tzŭ," or "Speech and Writing: Characters Untied," containing about ten thousand characters in their primitive and final forms. This work is on the desk of every scholar in the Far East and is studied with the greatest reverence. Many editions have appeared since it was written, and by its aid one can trace the genealogy of characters in the most complete manner. Other volumes of the same kind have followed in its wake, showing the importance of the subject in Chinese estimation. While translators are apt to ignore this matter of character genealogy, it is ever present to the mind of the Chinese poet or scholar who is familiar with the original forms; indeed, he may be said to find his overtones in the actual composition of the character he is using.

INTRODUCTION

All words have their connotations, but this is connotation and more; it is a pictorial representation of something implied, and, lacking which, an effect would be lost. It may be objected that poems were heard as well as read, and that, when heard, the composition of the character must be lost. But I think this is to misunderstand the situation. Recollect, for a moment, the literary examinations, and consider that educated men had these characters literally ground into them. Merely to pronounce a word must be, in such a case, to see it and realize, half-unconsciously perhaps, its various parts. Even if half-unconscious, the *nuances* of meaning conveyed by them must have hung about the spoken word and given it a distinct flavour which, without them, would be absent.

Now what is a translator to do? Shall he render the word in the flat, dictionary sense, or shall he permit himself to add to it what it conveys to an educated Chinese? Clearly neither the one nor the other in all cases; but one *or* the other, which the context must determine. In description, for instance, where it is evident that the Chinese poet used every means at his command to achieve a vivid representation, I believe the original poem is more nearly reproduced by availing one's self of a minimum of these "split-ups"; where, on the other hand, the original carefully confines itself to simple and direct expression, the word as it is, without overtones, must certainly be preferred. The

INTRODUCTION

"split-ups" in these translations are few, but could our readers compare the original Chinese with Miss Lowell's rendition of it, in these instances, I think they would feel with me that in no other way could the translation have been made really "literal," could the poem be "brought over" in its entirety. If a translation of a poem is not poetry in its new tongue, the original has been shorn of its chief reason for being. Something is always lost in a translation, but that something had better be the trappings than the essence.

I must, however, make it quite clear how seldom these "split-ups" occur in the principal parts of the book; in the "Written Pictures," where the poems were not, most of them, classics, we felt justified in making a fuller use of these analytical suggestions; but I believe I am correct in saying that no translations from the Chinese that I have read are so near to the originals as these. Bear in mind, then, that there are not, I suppose, more than a baker's dozen of these "split-ups" throughout the book, and the way they were managed can be seen by this literal translation of a line in "The Terraced Road of the Two-Edged Sword Mountains." The Chinese words are on the left, the English words on the right, the analyses of the characters enclosed in brackets:

INTRODUCTION

Shang Above
Tsê Then
Sung Pines
Fêng Wind
Hsiao Whistling wind (Grass — meaning the sound of wind through grass, to whistle; and in awe of, or to venerate.)
Sê Gusts of wind (Wind; and to stand.)
Sê A psaltery (Two strings of jade-stones which are sonorous.)
Yü Wind in a gale (Wind; and to speak.)

Miss Lowell's rendering of the line was:

"On their heights, the wind whistles awesomely in the pines; it booms in great, long gusts; it clashes like the strings of a jade-stone psaltery; it shouts on the clearness of a gale."

Can any one doubt that this was just the effect that the Chinese poet wished to achieve, and did achieve by means of the overtones given in his characters?

Another, simpler, example is in a case where the Chinese poet speaks of a rising sun. There are many characters which denote sunrise, and each has some shade of difference from every other. In one, the analysis is the sunrise light seen from a boat through mist; in another, it is the sun just above the horizon; still another is made up of a period of time and a mortar, meaning that it is dawn, when people begin to work. But the poet chose none of these; instead, he chose a character which analyzes into the sun at the height of a helmeted man, and so Miss Lowell speaks of

INTRODUCTION

the sun as "head-high," and we have the very picture the poet wanted us to see.

Miss Lowell has told in the Preface the manner in which we worked. The papers sent to Miss Lowell were in exactly the form of the above, and with them I also sent a paraphrase, and notes such as those at the end of this book. Far from making the slightest attempt at literary form in these paraphrases, I deliberately made them as bald as possible, and strove to keep my personality from intruding between Miss Lowell and the Chinese poet with whose mood she must be in perfect sympathy. Her remarkable gift for entering into the feeling of the poet she is translating was first shown in "Six French Poets," but there she approached her authors at first hand. It was my object to enable her to approach these Chinese authors as nearly at first hand as I could. That my method has been justified by the event, the book shows; not merely are these translations extraordinarily exact, they are poetry, and would be so though no Chinese poet had conceived them fourteen hundred years ago. It is as if I had handed her the warp and the woof, the silver threads and the gold, and from these she has woven a brocade as nearly alike in pattern to that designed by the Chinese poet as the differences in the looms permit. I believe that this is the first time that English translations of Chinese poetry have been made by a student of Chinese and a poet working together. Our ex-

INTRODUCTION

perience of the partnership has taught us both much; if we are pioneers in such a collaboration, we only hope that others will follow our lead.

The second section of the book, "Written Pictures," consists of illustrations, or half illustrations, of an art which the Chinese consider the most perfect medium in which a man can express himself. These *Tzŭ Hua*, "Hanging-on-the-Wall Poems," are less known and understood than any other form of Oriental art. A beautiful thought perpetuated in beautiful handwriting and hung upon the wall to suggest a mental picture — that is what it amounts to.

In China, the arts of poetry and calligraphy are united in the ideographs which form the written language. There are several different styles in which these ideographs, or characters, may be written. The earliest are pictograms known as the "ancient pictorial script," they were superseded in the Eighth Century B.C. by the "great seal" characters and later by the "lesser seal." These, which had been executed with the "knife pen," were practically given up when the invention of the writing-brush, which is usually translated as "pencil," revolutionized calligraphy (*circa* 215 B.C.). Their place was taken by a type of character known as "*li*" or "official script," a simplified form of the "seal," and this, being an improvement upon all previous styles, soon became popular. It created almost a new character in which the pictorial element had largely

INTRODUCTION

disappeared, and, with certain modifications, holds good to-day. The "model hand," the "running hand," and the famous "grass hand," so popular with poets and painters, are merely adaptations of the *li*; all three of these, together with the *li* itself, are used in the composition of written pictures.

The written pictures here translated were formerly in the possession of a Chinese gentleman of keenly æsthetic taste, and are excellent examples of the art. A photograph of one of the originals will be found opposite the translation made from it on page 170. The names which follow the poems are not those of the authors, but of the calligraphists. In the case of two poems, the authors' names are also given. These written pictures had no titles, those given here were added simply for convenience; but the titles to the poems in the body of the book are those of the poets themselves, except in one or two instances where the Chinese title conveyed so little to an Occidental mind that its meaning had to be paraphrased.

The Notes at the end of the book are intended for the general reader. For which reason, I have purposely excluded the type of note which consists in cataloguing literary cross-allusions. To know that certain lines in a poem are quoted from some earlier author, is one of a class of facts which deeply interest scholars, but are of no importance whatever to the rest of the world.

INTRODUCTION

A word as to the title of this book: There lived at Ch'êng-tu, the capital of Szechwan, early in the Ninth Century, a courtesan named Hsieh T'ao, who was famous for her wit and verse-writing. Hsieh T'ao made a paper of ten colours, which she dipped in a stream, and on it wrote her poems. Now, some years before, a woman had taken the stole of a Buddhist priest to this stream in order to wash it. No sooner had the stole touched the water than the stream became filled with flowers. In an old Chinese book, "The Treasury of Pleasant Records," it is told that, later in life, Hsieh T'ao gave up the "fir-flower tablets" and made paper of a smaller size. Presumably this fir-flower paper was the paper of ten colours. The mountain stream which ran near Hsieh T'ao's house is called the "Hundred Flower Stream."

I cannot close this Introduction without expressing my gratitude to my teacher, Mr. Nung Chu. It is his unflagging interest and never-failing patience that have kept me spurred on to my task. Speaking no word of English, Mr. Nung must often have found my explanations of what would, and what would not, be comprehensible to Occidental readers very difficult to understand, and my only regret is that he cannot read the book now that it is done.

FIR-FLOWER TABLETS

SONGS OF THE MARCHES
BY LI T'AI-PO

I

It is the Fifth Month,
But still the Heaven-high hills
Shine with snow.
There are no flowers
For the heart of the earth is yet too chilly.
From the centre of the camp
Comes the sound of a flute
Playing "The Snapped Willow."
No colour mists the trees,
Not yet have their leaves broken.
At dawn, there is the shock and shouting of battle,
Following the drums and the loud metal gongs.
At night, the soldiers sleep, clasping the pommels of their
    jade-ornamented saddles.
They sleep lightly,
With their two-edged swords girt below their loins,
So that they may be able in an instant to rush upon the
    Barbarians
And destroy them.

FIR-FLOWER TABLETS

II

Horses!
Horses!
Swift as the three dogs' wind!
Whips stinging the clear air like the sharp calling of birds,
They ride across the camel-back bridge
Over the river Wei.
They bend the bows,
Curving them away from the moon which shines behind them
Over their own country of Han.
They fasten feathers on their arrows
To destroy the immense arrogance of the foe.
Now the regiments are divided
And scattered like the five-pointed stars,
Sea mist envelops the deserted camp,
The task is accomplished,
And the portrait of Ho P'iao Yao
Hangs magnificently in the Lin Pavilion.

III

When Autumn burns along the hills,
The Barbarian hordes mount their horses
And pour down from the North.
Then, in the country of Han,
The Heavenly soldiers arise
And depart from their homes.

FIR-FLOWER TABLETS

The High General
Divides the tiger tally.
Fight, Soldiers!
Then lie down and rest
On the Dragon sand.
The frontier moon casts the shadows of bows upon the ground,
Swords brush the hoar-frost flowers of the Barbarians' country.
The Jade Pass has not yet been forced,
Our soldiers hold it strongly.
Therefore the young married women
May cease their lamentations.

IV

The Heavenly soldiers are returning
From the sterile plains of the North.
Because the Barbarians desired their horses
To drink of the streams of the South,
Therefore were our spears held level to the charge
In a hundred fights.
In straight battle our soldiers fought
To gain the supreme gratitude
Of the Most High Emperor.
They seized the snow of the Inland Sea
And devoured it in their terrible hunger.
They lay on the sand at the top of the Dragon Mound
And slept.

FIR-FLOWER TABLETS

All this they bore that the Moon Clan
Might be destroyed.
Now indeed have they won the right
To the soft, high bed of Peace.
It is their just portion.

THE BATTLE TO THE SOUTH OF THE CITY
BY LI T'AI-PO

How dim the battle-field, as yellow dusk!
The fighting men are like a swarm of ants.
The air is thick, the sun a red wheel.
Blood dyes the wild chrysanthemums purple.
Vultures hold the flesh of men in their mouths,
They are heavy with food — they cannot rise to fly.
There were men yesterday on the city wall;
There are ghosts to-day below the city wall.
Colours of flags like a net of stars,
Rolling of horse-carried drums — not yet is the killing ended.
From the house of the Unworthy One — a husband, sons,
All within earshot of the rolling horse-drums.

THE PERILS OF THE SHU ROAD
BY LI T'AI-PO

ALAS! Alas! The danger! The steepness! O Affliction!
The Shu Road is as perilous and difficult as the way to the Green Heavens.
No greater undertaking than this has been since Ts'an Ts'ung and Yü Fu ruled the land.
For forty-eight thousand years no man had passed the boundary of Ch'in.
Westward, over the Great White Mountain, was a bird-track
By which one could cross to the peak of Omei.
But the earth of the mountain fell and overwhelmed the Heroes so that they perished.
Afterwards, therefore, they made sky-ladders and joined the cliffs with hanging pathways.
Above, the soaring tips of the high mountains hold back the six dragons of the sun;
Below, in the ravines, the flowing waters break into whirlpools and swirl back against the current.
Yellow geese flying toward the peaks cannot pass over them;
The gibbons climb and climb, despairingly pulling themselves up higher and higher, but even their endurance fails.

FIR-FLOWER TABLETS

How the road coils and coils through the Green Mud Pass!
With nine turns to a hundred steps, it winds round the ledges of the mountain crests.
Clutching at Orion, passing the Well Star, I look up and gasp.
I sit long with my hand pressed to my heart and groan.
I ask my Lord how long this Westward wandering will last, when we shall return.
It is impossible to climb the terrible road along the edges of the precipices.
Among the ancient trees, one sees only cruel, mournful, black birds.
Male birds, followed by females, fly to and fro through the woods.
Sometimes one hears a nightingale in the melancholy moonlight of the lonely mountain.
The Shu Road is as perilous and difficult as the way to the Green Heavens.
The ruddy faces of those who hear the story of it turn pale.
There is not a cubit's space between the mountain tops and the sky.
Dead and uprooted pine-trees hang over sheer cliffs.
Flying waterfalls and rolling torrents outdo one another in clamour and confusion;
They dash against the perpendicular walls, whirl round ten thousand rocks, and boom like thunder along the ravines.

This is what the Two-Edged Sword Mountains are like!
Alas! How endless a road for man to undertake! How came he to attempt it!
The Terraced Road of the Two-Edged Sword twists between glittering and rocky summits.
One man alone could hold it against a thousand and mow them down like grass.
If the guardian of the Pass were doubtful whether those who came were enemies of his kinsmen,
He could fall upon them as a ravening wolf.
At dawn, one flees the fierce tigers;
In the evening, one flees the long snakes
Who sharpen their fangs and suck blood,
Destroying men like hemp.
Even though the delights of the Embroidered City are as reported,
Nothing could equal the joy of going home at once.
The Shu Road is as perilous and difficult as the way to the Green Heavens.
I turn toward the West, and, gazing long, I sigh.

LOOKING AT THE MOON AFTER RAIN
BY LI T'AI-PO

THE heavy clouds are broken and blowing,
And once more I can see the wide common stretching beyond the four sides of the city.
Open the door. Half of the moon-toad is already up,
The glimmer of it is like smooth hoar-frost spreading over ten thousand *li*.
The river is a flat, shining chain.
The moon, rising, is a white eye to the hills;
After it has risen, it is the bright heart of the sea.
Because I love it — so — round as a fan,
I hum songs until the dawn.

THE LONELY WIFE
BY LI T'AI-PO

THE mist is thick. On the wide river, the water-plants float smoothly.
No letters come; none go.
There is only the moon, shining through the clouds of a hard, jade-green sky,
Looking down at us so far divided, so anxiously apart.
All day, going about my affairs, I suffer and grieve, and press the thought of you closely to my heart.
My eyebrows are locked in sorrow, I cannot separate them.
Nightly, nightly, I keep ready half the quilt,
And wait for the return of that divine dream which is my Lord.

Beneath the quilt of the Fire-Bird, on the bed of the Silver-Crested Love-Pheasant,
Nightly, nightly, I drowse alone.
The red candles in the silver candlesticks melt, and the wax runs from them,
As the tears of your so Unworthy One escape and continue constantly to flow.
A flower face endures but a short season,
Yet still he drifts along the river Hsiao and the river Hsiang.

FIR-FLOWER TABLETS

As I toss on my pillow, I hear the cold, nostalgic sound of the water-clock:
Shêng! Shêng! it drips, cutting my heart in two.

I rise at dawn. In the Hall of Pictures
They come and tell me that the snow-flowers are falling.
The reed-blind is rolled high, and I gaze at the beautiful, glittering, primeval snow,
Whitening the distance, confusing the stone steps and the courtyard.
The air is filled with its shining, it blows far out like the smoke of a furnace.
The grass-blades are cold and white, like jade girdle pendants.
Surely the Immortals in Heaven must be crazy with wine to cause such disorder,
Seizing the white clouds, crumpling them up, destroying them.

THE PLEASURES WITHIN THE PALACE
BY LI T'AI-PO

FROM little, little girls, they have lived in the Golden House.
They are lovely, lovely, in the Purple Hall.
They dress their hair with hill flowers,
And rock-bamboos are embroidered on their dresses of open-work silk gauze.
When they go out from the retired Women's Apartments,
They often follow the Palace chairs.
Their only sorrow, that the songs and wu dances are over,
Changed into the five-coloured clouds and flown away.

THE YOUNG GIRLS OF YÜEH
BY LI T'AI-PO

I

Young girls are gathering lotus-seeds on the pond of Ya.
Seeing a man on the bank, they turn and row away singing.
Laughing, they hide among the lotus-flowers,
And, in a pretence of bashfulness, will not come out.

II

Many of the young girls of Wu are white, dazzlingly white.
They like to amuse themselves by floating in little boats on the water.
Peeping out of the corners of their eyes, they spurn the Springtime heart.
Gathering flowers, they ridicule the passer-by.

WRITTEN IN THE CHARACTER OF A BEAUTIFUL WOMAN GRIEVING BEFORE HER MIRROR
BY LI T'AI-PO

I

BRIGHT, bright, the gilded magpie mirror,
Absolutely perfect in front of me on the jade dressing-stand.
Wiped, rubbed, splendid as the Winter moon;
Its light and brilliance, how clear and round!
The rose-red face is older than it was yesterday,
The hair is whiter than it was last year.
The white-lead powder is neglected,
It is useless to look into the mirror. I am utterly miserable.

II

When my Lord went away, he gave me this precious mirror coiled with dragons
That I might gaze at my golden-threaded dress of silken gauze.
Again and again I take my red sleeve and polish the bright moon,
Because I love to see its splendour lighting up everything.
In its centre is my reflection, and the golden magpie which does not fly away.

FIR-FLOWER TABLETS

I sit at my dressing-stand, and I am like the green Fire-Bird who, thinking of its mate, died alone.
My husband is parted from me as an arrow from the bow-string.
I know the day he left; I do not know the year when he will return.
The cruel wind blows — truly the heart of the Unworthy One is cut to pieces.
My tears, like white jade chop-sticks, fall in a single piece before the water-chestnut mirror.

SONGS TO THE PEONIES SUNG TO THE AIR: "PEACEFUL BRIGHTNESS"
BY LI T'AI-PO

I

The many-coloured clouds make me think of her upper garments, of her lower garments;
Flowers make me think of her face.
The Spring wind brushes the blossoms against the balustrade,
In the heavy dew they are bright and tinted diversely.
If it were not on the Heaped Jade Mountain that I saw her,
I must have met her at the Green Jasper Terrace, or encountered her by accident in the moon.

II

A branch of opulent, beautiful flowers, sweet-scented under frozen dew.
No love-night like that on the Sorceress Mountain for these; their bowels ache in vain.
Pray may I ask who, in the Palace of Han, is her equal?
Even the "Flying Swallow" is to be pitied, since she must rely upon ever new adornments.

III

The renowned flower, and she of a loveliness to overthrow Kingdoms— both give happiness.

FIR-FLOWER TABLETS

Each receives a smile from the Prince when he looks at them.
The Spring wind alone can understand and explain the boundless jealousy of the flower,
Leaning over the railing of the balcony at the North side of the aloe-wood pavilion.

SPRING GRIEF AND RESENTMENT
BY LI T'AI-PO

There is a white horse with a gold bridle to the East of the Liao Sea.
Bed-curtains of open-work silk — embroidered quilt — I sleep with the Spring wind.
The setting moon drops level to the balcony, it spies upon me. The candle is burnt out.
A blown flower drifts in through the inner door — it mocks at the empty bed.

THE CAST–OFF PALACE WOMAN OF CH'IN AND THE DRAGON ROBES
BY LI T'AI-PO

At Wei Yang dwells the Son of Heaven.
The all Unworthy One attends beside
The Dragon-broidered robes.
I ponder his regard, not mine the love
Enjoyed by those within the Purple Palace.
And yet I have attained to brightening
The bed of yellow gold.
If floods should come, I also would not leave.
A bear might come and still I could protect.
My inconsiderable body knows the honour
Of serving Sun and Moon.
I flicker with a little glow of light,
A firefly's. I beg my Lord to pluck
The trifling mustard plant and melon-flower
And not reject them for their hidden roots.

THE POET IS DETAINED IN A NANKING WINE-SHOP ON THE EVE OF STARTING ON A JOURNEY
BY LI T'AI-PO

THE wind blows. The inn is filled with the scent of willow-flowers.
In the wine-shops of Wu, women are pressing the wine. The sight invites customers to taste.
The young men and boys of Nanking have gathered to see me off;
I wish to start, but I do not, and we drink many, many horn cups to the bottom.
I beg them to look at the water flowing toward the East,
And when we separate to let their thoughts follow its example and run constantly in my direction.

FÊNG HUANG T'AI

ASCENDING THE TERRACE OF THE SILVER-CRESTED LOVE-PHEASANTS AT THE CITY OF THE GOLDEN MOUND

BY LI T'AI-PO

THE silver-crested love-pheasants strutted upon the Pheasant Terrace.
Now the pheasants are gone, the terrace is empty, and the river flows on its old, original way.
Gone are the blossoms of the Palace of Wu and overgrown the road to it.
Passed the generations of the Chin, with their robes and head-dresses; they lie beneath the ancient mounds.

The three hills are half fallen down from Green Heaven.
The White Heron Island cuts the river in two.
Here also, drifting clouds may blind the Sun,
One cannot see Ch'ang An, City of Eternal Peace.
  Therefore am I sorrowful.

THE NORTHERN FLIGHT
BY LI T'AI-PO

WHAT hardships are encountered in a Northern flight!
We fly Northward, ascending the T'ai Hang Mountains.
The mountain road winds round a cliff, and it is very steep and dangerous;
The precipice, sheer as though cut with a knife, rises to the great, wide blue of the sky.
The horses' feet slip on the slanting ledges;
The carriage-wheels are broken on the high ridges;
The sand, scuffed into dust, floats in a continuous line to Yo Chou.
The smoke of beacon fires connects us with the Country of the North.
The spirit of killing is in the spears, in the cruel two-edged swords.
The savage wind rips open the upper garments, the lower garments.
The rushing whale squeezes the Yellow River;
The man-eating beasts with long tusks assemble at Lo Yang.

We press forward with no knowledge of when we shall return;
We look back, thinking of our former home;

Grieving and lamenting in the midst of ice and snow;
Groaning aloud, with our bowels rent asunder.
A foot of cloth does not cover the body,
Our skins are cracked as the bark of a dead mulberry.
The deep gullies prevent us from getting water from the mountain streams,
Far away are the slopes where we might gather grass and twigs for our fires,
Then, too, the terrible tiger lashes his tail,
And his polished teeth glitter like Autumn frosts.
Grass and trees cannot be eaten.
We famish; we drink the drops of freezing dew.
Alas! So we suffer, travelling Northward.
I stop my four-horse carriage, overcome by misery.
When will our Emperor find a peaceful road?
When, before our glad faces, shall we see the Glory of Heaven?

FIGHTING TO THE SOUTH OF THE CITY
BY LI T'AI-PO

Last year they fought at the source of the Sang Ch'ien,
This year they fight on the road by the Leek-green River.
The soldiers were drenched by the waters of the Aral Sea,
The horses were turned loose to find grass in the midst of the snows of the Heaven High Hills.
Over ten thousand *li*, they attacked and fought,
The three divisions are crumbled, decayed, utterly worn and old.
The Hsiung Nu use killing and slaughter in the place of the business of plowing.
From ancient times, only dry, white bones are seen on the yellow sand-fields.
The House of Ch'in erected and pounded firm the wall to make a barrier before the dwelling-place of the Barbarians,
The House of Han still preserved the beacon-stands where fires are lighted.
The lighting of beacon fires on the stands never ceases,
The fighting and attacking are without a time of ending.
In savage attack they die — fighting without arms.
The riderless horses scream with terror, throwing their heads up to the sky.

Vultures and kites tear the bowels of men with their beaks
And fly to hang them on the branches of dead trees.
Officers and soldiers lying in mud, in grass, in undergrowth.
Helpless, the General — Yes, incapable before this!
We have learnt that soldiers are evil tools,
But wise men have not accomplished the ending of war, and
    still we employ them.

THE CROSSWISE RIVER
BY LI T'AI-PO

I

THERE are people who say the Crosswise River is good;
I say the Crosswise River is terrible.
The savage wind blows as if it would overturn the Heaven's Gate Mountains.
The white waves are as high as the high rooms in the Temple of Wa Kuan.

II

The sea tide flowing Southward passes Hsün Yang.
From the beginning of things, the Ox Ledge has been more dangerous than the Standing Horse Hill.
Those who wish to cross the Crosswise River
Find evil winds and waves.
The misery of that one stretch of water draws out its length to ten thousand *li*.

III

When the Sea Demon passes by, a vicious wind curves back.
The waves beat open the rock wall of the Gate of Heaven.
Is the Eighth Month tide-bore of Chêkiang equal to this?
It seems as though the vast, booming waves were part of the mountains — they spurt out snow.

ON HEARING THE BUDDHIST PRIEST OF SHU PLAY HIS TABLE-LUTE
BY LI T'AI-PO

THE Priest of the Province of Shu, carrying his table-lute in
    a cover of green, shot silk,
Comes down the Western slope of the peak of Mount Omei.
He moves his hands for me, striking the lute.
It is like listening to the waters in ten thousand ravines, and
    the wind in ten thousand pine-trees.
The traveller's heart is washed clean as in flowing water.
The echoes of the overtones join with the evening bell.
I am not conscious of the sunset behind the jade-grey hill,
Nor how many and dark are the Autumn clouds.

CH'ANG KAN

BY LI T'AI-PO

When the hair of your Unworthy One first began to cover her forehead,
She picked flowers and played in front of the door.
Then you, my Lover, came riding a bamboo horse.
We ran round and round the bed, and tossed about the sweetmeats of green plums.
We both lived in the village of Ch'ang Kan.
We were both very young, and knew neither jealousy nor suspicion.
At fourteen, I became the wife of my Lord.
I could not yet lay aside my face of shame;
I hung my head, facing the dark wall;
You might call me a thousand times, not once would I turn round.
At fifteen, I stopped frowning.
I wanted to be with you, as dust with its ashes.
I often thought that you were the faithful man who clung to the bridge-post,
That I should never be obliged to ascend to the Looking-for-Husband Ledge.
When I was sixteen, my Lord went far away,
To the Ch'ü T'ang Chasm and the Whirling Water Rock of the Yü River

Which, during the Fifth Month, must not be collided with;
Where the wailing of the gibbons seems to come from the sky.
Your departing footprints are still before the door where I
 bade you good-bye,
In each has sprung up green moss.
The moss is thick, it cannot be swept away.
The leaves are falling, it is early for the Autumn wind to
 blow.
It is the Eighth Month, the butterflies are yellow,
Two are flying among the plants in the West garden;
Seeing them, my heart is bitter with grief, they wound the
 heart of the Unworthy One.
The bloom of my face has faded, sitting with my sorrow.
From early morning until late in the evening, you descend
 the Three Serpent River.
Prepare me first with a letter, bringing me the news of when
 you will reach home.
I will not go far on the road to meet you,
I will go straight until I reach the Long Wind Sands.

SORROW DURING A CLEAR AUTUMN
BY LI T'AI-PO

I CLIMB the hills of Chiu I — Oh-h-h-h-h! I look at the clear streams a long way off.
I see distinctly the three branches of the Hsiang River, I hear the sound of its swift current.
The water flows coldly; it is on its way to the lake.
The horizontal Autumn clouds hide the sky.
I go by the "Bird's Path." I calculate the distance to my old home. Oh-h-h-h-h!
I do not know how many thousand *li* it is from Ching to Wu.
It is the hour of the Western brightness, of the half-round sun.
The dazzle on the island is about to disappear;
The smooth lake is brilliantly white — from the moon?
Over the lake, the moon is rising.
I think of the moment of meeting — the long stretch of time before it.
I think of misty Yen and gaze at Yüeh.
The lotus-flowers have fallen — Oh-h-h-h-h! The river is the colour of Autumn.
The wind passes — passes. The night is endless — endless.
I would go to the end of the Dark Sea. How eagerly I desire this!

FIR-FLOWER TABLETS

I think much of fishing for a leviathan from the Island of
    the Cold Sea.
There is no rod long enough to raise it.
I yield to the great waves, and my sorrow is increased.
I will return. I will go home. Oh-h-h-h-h!
Even for a little time, one cannot rely upon the World.
I long to pick the immortal herbs on the hill of P'êng.

POIGNANT GRIEF DURING A SUNNY SPRING
BY LI T'AI-PO

The East wind has come again.
I see the jade-green grass and realize that it is Spring.
Everywhere there is an immense confusion of ripples and agitations.
Why does the waving and fluttering of the weeping-willow make me sad?
The sky is so bright it shines; everything is lovely and at peace.
The breath of the sea is green, fresh, sweet-smelling;
The heaths are vari-coloured, blue — green — as a kingfisher feather. Oh-h-h-h-h — How far one can see!
Clouds whirl, fly, float, and cluster together, each one sharply defined;
Waves are smoothed into a wide, continuous flowing.
I examine the young moss in the well, how it starts into life.
I see something dim — Oh-h-h-h-h — waving up and down like floss silk.
I see it floating — it is a cobweb, coiling like smoke.
Before all these things — Oh-h-h-h-h — my soul is severed from my body.
Confronted with the wind, the brilliance, I suffer.

I feel as one feels listening to the sound of the waters of the
    Dragon Mound in Ch'in,
The gibbons wailing by the Serpent River.
I feel as the "Shining One" felt when she passed the Jade
    Frontier,
As the exile of Ch'u in the Maple Forest.
I will try to climb a high hill and look far away into the
    distance.
Pain cuts me to the bone and wounds my heart.
My Spring heart is agitated as the surface of the sea,
My Spring grief is bewildered like a flurry of snow.
Ten thousand emotions are mingled — their sorrow and their
    joy.
Yet I know only that my heart is torn in this Spring season.
She of whom I am thinking — Oh-h-h-h-h — is at the shore
    of the Hsiang River,
Separated by the clouds and the rainbow — without these
    mists I could surely see.
I scatter my tears a foot's length upon the water's surface.
I entrust the Easterly flowing water with my passion for the
    Cherished One.
If I could command the shining of the Spring, could grasp it
    without putting it out — Oh-h-h-h-h —
I should wish to send it as a gift to that beautiful person at
    the border of Heaven.

TWO POEMS WRITTEN AS PARTING GIFTS TO TS'UI (THE OFFICIAL) OF CH'IU PU

BY LI T'AI-PO

I LOVE Ts'ui of Ch'iu Pu.
He follows the ways of the Official T'ao.
At his gate, he has planted five willow-trees,
And on either side of the well, crowding it between them,
    stand two wu-t'ung trees.
Mountain birds fly down and listen while he transacts business;
From the eaves of his house, flowers drop into the midst of
    his wine.
Thinking of my Lord, I cannot bear to depart.
My thoughts are melancholy and endless.

II

My Lord is like T'ao of P'êng Tsê.
Often, during the day, he sleeps at the North window.
Again, in the moonlight, he bends over his table-lute and
    plays,
His hands follow his thoughts, for there are no strings.
When a guest comes, it is wine alone which he pours out.
He is the best of officials, since he does not care for gold.
He has planted many grains on the Eastern heights,
And he admonishes all the people to plow their fields early.

SENT AS A PARTING GIFT TO THE SECOND OFFICIAL OF CH'IU PU

BY LI T'AI-PO

In the old days, Ch'iu Pu was bare and desolate,
The serving-men in the Official Residence were few.
Because you, my Lord, have planted peach-trees and plum-trees,
This place has suddenly become exuberantly fragrant.
As your writing-brush moves, making the characters so full of life, you gaze at the white clouds;
And, when the reed-blinds are rolled up, at the kingfisher-green of the fading hills;
And, when the time comes, for long at the mountain moon;
Still again, when you are exhilarated with wine, at the shadow of the moon in the wine-cup.
Great man and teacher, I love you.
I linger.
I cannot bear to leave.

THE SONG OF THE WHITE CLOUDS

SAYING GOOD-BYE TO LIU SIXTEEN ON HIS RETURN TO THE HILLS

BY LI T'AI-PO

The hills of Ch'u,
The hills of Ch'in,
White clouds everywhere.
White clouds follow my Lord always,
From place to place. They always follow
My Lord,
When my Lord arrives at the hills of Ch'u.
Clouds also follow my Lord when he floats
In a boat on the river Hsiang,
With the wild wistaria hanging above
The waters of the river Hsiang.
My Lord will go back
To where he can sleep
Among the white clouds,
When the sun is as high
As the head of a helmeted man.

WIND-BOUND AT THE NEW FOREST REACH.
A LETTER SENT TO A FRIEND
BY LI T'AI-PO

TIDAL water is a determined thing, it can be depended on;
But it is impossible to make an appointment with the wind
  of Heaven.
In the clear dawn, it veers Northwest;
At the last moment of sunset, it blows Southeast.
It is therefore difficult to set our sail.
The thought of our happy meeting becomes insistent.
The wide water reflects a moon no longer round, but broken.
Water grass springs green in the broad reach.
Yesterday, at the North Lake, there were plum-flowers;
They were just beginning to open, the branches were not
  covered.
To-day, at dawn, see the willows beyond the White Gate;
The road is squeezed between them, they drop down their
  bright green silk threads.
Everything stirs like this, with the year—
When will my coming be fixed?
Willow-blossoms lie thick as snow on the river,
I am worried, the heart of the traveller is sad.
"At daybreak I will leave the New Forest Reach"—
But what is the use of humming Hsieh T'iao's poem.

IN THE PROVINCE OF LU, AT THE ANCESTRAL SHRINE OF KING YAO. SAYING FAREWELL TO WU FIVE ON HIS DEPARTURE FOR LANG YA

BY LI T'AI-PO

KING YAO has been dead for three thousand years,
But the green pine, the ancient temple, remain.
As we are bidding you good-bye, we set out offerings of cassia wine;
We make obeisance, we bend our knees, and, rising, turn our faces to Heaven. Our hearts and spirits are pure.
The colour of the sun urges our return.
Song follows song, we tip up the flagon of sweet-scented wine.
The horses whinny. We are all tipsy, yet we rise.
Our hands separate. What words are there still to say?

DRINKING ALONE IN THE MOONLIGHT
BY LI T'AI-PO

I

A POT of wine among flowers.
I alone, drinking, without a companion.
I lift the cup and invite the bright moon.
My shadow opposite certainly makes us three.
But the moon cannot drink,
And my shadow follows the motions of my body in vain.
For the briefest time are the moon and my shadow my companions.
Oh, be joyful! One must make the most of Spring.
I sing — the moon walks forward rhythmically;
I dance, and my shadow shatters and becomes confused.
In my waking moments, we are happily blended.
When I am drunk, we are divided from one another and scattered.
For a long time I shall be obliged to wander without intention;
But we will keep our appointment by the far-off Cloudy River.

DRINKING ALONE IN THE MOONLIGHT
BY LI T'AI-PO
II

If Heaven did not love wine,
There would be no Wine Star in Heaven.
If Earth did not love wine,
There should be no Wine Springs on Earth.
Why then be ashamed before Heaven to love wine.
I have heard that clear wine is like the Sages;
Again it is said that thick wine is like the Virtuous Worthies.
Wherefore it appears that we have swallowed both Sages and Worthies.
Why should we strive to be Gods and Immortals?
Three cups, and one can perfectly understand the Great Tao;
A gallon, and one is in accord with all nature.
Only those in the midst of it can fully comprehend the joys of wine;
I do not proclaim them to the sober.

A STATEMENT OF RESOLUTIONS AFTER BEING DRUNK ON A SPRING DAY
BY LI T'AI-PO

This time of ours
Is like a great, confused dream.
Why should one spend one's life in toil?
Thinking this, I have been drunk all day.
I fell down and lay prone by the pillars in front of the house;
When I woke up, I gazed for a long time
At the courtyard before me.
A bird sings among the flowers.
May I ask what season this is?
Spring wind,
The bright oriole of the water-flowing flight calls.
My feelings make me want to sigh.
The wine is still here, I will throw back my head and drink.

I sing splendidly,
I wait for the bright moon.
Already, by the end of the song, I have forgotten my feelings.

RIVER CHANT

BY LI T'AI-PO

F<small>IG-WOOD</small> oars,
A boat of the wood of the sand-pear.
At either end,
Jade flageolets and pipes of gold.

Amidships,
Jars of delectable wine,
And ten thousand pints
Put by.

A boat-load of singing-girls
Following the water ripples —
Going,
Stopping,
Veering —

The Immortal waited,
Then mounted and rode the yellow crane.
But he who is the guest of the sea has no such desire,
Rather would he be followed by the white gulls.

The *tzŭ* and *fu* of Ch'ü P'ing hang suspended like the sun
    and moon.
The terraces and the pleasure-houses

Of the Kings of Ch'u
Are empty heaps of earth.

I am drunk with wine,
With the sweet taste of it;
I am overflowed with the joy of it.
When I take up my writing-brush,
I could move the Five Peaks.

When I have finished my poem,
I laugh aloud in my arrogance.
I rise to the country of the Immortals which lies in the middle of the sea.
If fame followed the ways of the good official,
If wealth and rank were long constant,
Then indeed might the water of the Han River flow Northwest.

SEPARATED BY IMPERIAL SUMMONS FROM HER WHO LIVES WITHIN

BY LI T'AI-PO

I

The Emperor commands; three times the summons. He who left has not yet returned.
To-morrow, at sunrise, he will go out by the Pass of Wu.
From the upper chamber of white jade, I shall gaze far off; but I shall be able to make out nothing.
Our thoughts will be with each other. I must ascend the Looking-for-Husband Hill.

II

As I left my door, my wife dragged my clothes with all her strength.
She asked me in how many days I should return from the West.
"When I return, supposing I wear at my girdle the yellow gold seal,
You must not imitate Su Ch'in's wife and not leave your loom."

III

The upper chamber of kingfisher jade, the stairs of gold —
Who passes the night alone, leaning against the door and sobbing?

She sits all night by the cold lamp until the moon melts into the dawn.
Her streaming, streaming tears are exhausted — to the West of the Ch'u Barrier.

A WOMAN SINGS TO THE AIR: "SITTING AT NIGHT"

BY LI T'AI-PO

A Winter night, a cold Winter night. To me, the night is unending.
I chant heavily to myself a long time. I sit, sit in the North Hall.
The water in the well is solid with ice. The moon enters the Women's Apartments.
The flame of the gold lamp is very small, the oil is frozen.
It shines on the misery of my weeping.

The gold lamp goes out,
But the weeping continues and increases.
The Unworthy One hides her tears in her sleeve.
She hearkens to the song of her Lord, to the sound of it.
The Unworthy One knows her passion.
The passion and the sound unite,
There is no discord between them.
If a single phrase were unsympathetic to my thoughts,
Then, though my Lord sang ten thousand verses which should cause even the dust on the beams to fly, to me it would be nothing.

THE PALACE WOMAN OF HAN TAN BECOMES THE WIFE OF THE SOLDIERS' COOK
BY LI T'AI-PO

ONCE the Unworthy One was a maiden of the Ts'ung Terrace.
Joyfully lifting my moth-pencilled eyebrows, I entered the carnation-coloured Palace.
Relying on myself, my flower-like face,
How should I know that it would wither and fade?
Banished below the jade steps,
Gone as the early morning clouds are gone,
Whenever I think of Han Tan City
I dream of the Autumn moon from the middle of the Palace.
I cannot see the Prince, my Lord.
Desolate, my longing — until daylight comes.

THE SORREL HORSE
BY LI T'AI-PO

The sorrel horse with the black tail gallops, gallops, and neighs,
Lifting, curving, his grey-jade hoofs.
He shies from the flowing water, unwilling to cross,
As though he feared the mud for his embroidered saddle-cloth.
The snow is white on the far frontier hills,
The clouds are yellow over the misty frontier sea.
I strike with my leather whip, there are ten thousand *li* to go.
How can I accomplish it, thinking of Spring in the Women's Apartments?

A POEM GIVEN TO A BEAUTIFUL WOMAN ENCOUNTERED ON A FIELD-PATH

BY LI T'AI-PO

The magnificent horse, galloping swiftly, tramples the fallen flower.
Down comes the riding-whip, straight down — it strikes the Five Cloud Cart.
The young person who lifts the pearl door-screen is very beautiful. Moreover, she smiles.
She points to a Red Building in the distance — it is the home of the Flower Maiden.

SAYING GOOD-BYE TO A FRIEND
BY LI T'AI-PO

CLEAR green hills at a right angle to the North wall,
White water winding to the East of the city.
Here is the place where we must part.
The lonely water-plants go ten thousand *li*;
The floating clouds wander everywhither as does man.
Day is departing — it and my friend.
Our hands separate. Now he is going.
"Hsiao, hsiao," the horse neighs.
He neighs again, "Hsiao, hsiao."

DESCENDING THE EXTREME SOUTH MOUNTAIN; PASSING THE HOUSE OF HU SSŬ, LOVER OF HILLS; SPENDING THE NIGHT IN THE PREPARATION OF WINE

BY LI T'AI-PO

We come down the green-grey jade hill,
The mountain moon accompanies us home.
We turn and look back up the path:
Green, green, the sky; the horizontal, kingfisher-green line of the hills is fading.
Holding each other's hands, we reach the house in the fields.
Little boys throw open the gate of thorn branches,
The quiet path winds among dark bamboos,
Creepers, bright with new green, brush our garments.
Our words are happy, rest is in them.
Of an excellent flavour, the wine! We scatter the dregs of it contentedly.
We sing songs for a long time; we chant them to the wind in the pine-trees.
By the time the songs are finished, the stars in Heaven's River are few.
I am tipsy. My friend is continuously merry.
In fact, we are so exhilarated that we both forget this complicated machine, the world.

THE TERRACED ROAD OF THE TWO-EDGED SWORD MOUNTAINS

BY LI T'AI-PO

LOOKING South and straight from Hsien Yang for five thousand *li*,
One could see, among the full, blowing clouds, the rocky sharpness of peaks,
Were it not for the horizontal line of the Two-Edged Sword Mountains cutting across the view.
They are flat against the green sky, and open in the middle to let the sky through.
On their heights, the wind whistles awesomely in the pines; it booms in great, long gusts; it clashes like the strings of a jade-stone psaltery; it shouts on the clearness of a gale.
In the Serpent River country, the gibbons — Oh-h-h-h-h — all the gibbons together moan and grieve.
Beside the road, torrents flung from a great height rush down the gully,
They toss stones and spray over the road, they run rapidly, they whirl, they startle with the noise of thunder.
I bid good-bye to my devoted friend — Oh-h-h-h-h — now he leaves me.
When will he come again? Oh-h-h-h-h — When will he return to me?

I hope for my dear friend the utmost peace.
My voice is heavy, I sigh and draw my breath haltingly.
I look at the green surface of the water flowing to the East.
I grieve that the white sun hides in the West.
The wild goose has taken the place of the swallow —
    Oh-h-h-h-h — I hear the pattering, falling noises of
    Autumn.
Dark are the rain clouds; the colour of the town of Ch'in
    is dark.
When the moon glistens on the Road of the Two-Edged
    Sword — Oh-h-h-h-h —
I and you, even though in different provinces, may drink
    our wine opposite each other,
And listen to the talking
Of our hearts.

HEARING A BAMBOO FLUTE ON A SPRING NIGHT IN THE CITY OF LO YANG

BY LI T'AI-PO

From whose house do the invisible notes of a jade flute come flying?
The Spring wind scatters them. They fill the City of Lo Yang.
To-night, as the phrases form, I hear "The Snapped Willow."
To whom do they not bring back the love of his old, early garden?

THE RETREAT OF HSIEH KUNG
BY LI T'AI-PO

The sun is setting — has set — on the Spring-green Mountain.
Hsieh Kung's retreat is solitary and still.
No sound of man in the bamboo grove.
The white moon shines in the centre of the unused garden pool.
All round the ruined Summer-house is decaying grass,
Grey mosses choke the abandoned well.
There is only the free, clear wind
Again — again — passing over the stones of the spring.

A TRAVELLER COMES TO THE OLD TERRACE OF SU

BY LI T'AI-PO

The old Imperial Park — the ruined Terrace — the young willows.
The water-chestnut pickers are singing, a simple song unaccompanied by instruments — but joy is unbearable.
For now the moon over the Western River is alone.
The time is past when she gazed upon the concubines in the Palace of the King of Wu.

THEME OF THE REST-HOUSE ON THE CLEAR WAN RIVER
BY LI T'AI-PO

I LOVE the beauty of the Wan River.
One can see its clear heart shining a hundred feet deep.
In what way does it not equal the river Hsin An?
For a thousand times eight feet one can see its bright bed,
The white sand keeps the colour of the moon.
The dark green bamboos accentuate the Autumn sounds.
Really one cannot help laughing to think that, until now,
    the rapid current celebrated by Yen
Has usurped all the fame.

DRINKING SONG
BY LI T'AI-PO

Do you not see the waters of the Yellow River coming down
 from Heaven?
They rush with incredible speed to the sea, and they never
 turn and come back again.
Do you not see, in the clear mirror of the Guest Hall, the
 miserable white hair on my head?
At dawn it is like shining thread, but at sunset it is snow.
In this life, to be perfectly happy, one must drain one's
 pleasures;
The golden wine-cup must not stand empty opposite the
 moon.
Heaven put us here, we must use what we have.
Scatter a thousand ounces of silver and you are but where
 you were.
Boil the sheep,
Kill the ox,
Be merry.
We should drink three hundred cups at once.
Mr. Wise Gentleman Ts'en,
And you, Mr. Scholar Tan Ch'iu,
Drink, you must not stop.
I will sing one of my poems for you,
Please lean over and listen:

"Bells! Drums! Delicacies
Worth their weight in jade —
These things
Are of the slightest value.
I only want to be drunk
For ages and never wake.
The sages and worthies of old times
Have left not a sound,
Only those who drank
Have achieved lasting fame.
The King of Ch'ên, long ago, caroused
In the Hall of Peaceful Content.
They drank wine paid
At a full ten thousand a gallon;
They surpassed themselves in mirth,
And the telling of obscene stories.
How can a host say
He has very little money.
It is absolutely imperative
That he buy wine for his friends.
Horses of five colours, dappled flower horses,
Fur coats costing
A thousand ounces of silver —
He sends his son to exchange
All these for delectable wine,
So that you and I together
May drown our ancient grief."

ANSWER TO AN AFFECTIONATE INVITATION FROM TS'UI FIFTEEN

BY LI T'AI-PO

You have the " bird's foot-print " characters.
You suggest that we drink together at the Lute Stream.
The characters you wrote are in the centre of a foot of pure white silk,
They are like exquisite clouds dropped from Heaven.
Having finished reading, I smile at the empty air,
I feel as though my friend were before me
Reciting verses for a long time.
The characters are not faded. I shall keep them in my sleeve, and they should last three years.

PARROT ISLAND
BY LI T'AI-PO

THE parrots come, they cross the river waters of Wu.
The island in the river is called Parrot Island.
The parrots are flying West to the Dragon Mountain.
There are sweet grasses on the island, and how green, green, are its trees!

The mists part and one can see the leaves of the spear-orchid, and its scent is warm on the wind;
The water is embroidered and shot with the reflections of the peach-tree blossoms growing on both banks.
Now indeed does the departing official realize the full meaning of his banishment.
The long island — the solitary moon — facing each other in the brightness.

THE HONOURABLE LADY CHAO
BY LI T'AI-PO

MOON over the houses of Han, over the site of Ch'in.
It flows as water — its brightness shone on Ming Fei, the
    "Bright Concubine,"
Who took the road to the Jade Pass.
She went to the edge of Heaven, but she did not return;
She gave up the moon of Han, she departed from the Eastern Sea.
The "Bright Concubine" married in the West, and the day
    of her returning never came.
For her beautiful painted face, there was the long, cold snow
    instead of flowers.
She, with eyebrows like the antennæ of moths, pined and
    withered.
Her grave is in the sand of the Barbarians' country.
Because, when alive, she did not pay out yellow gold,
The portrait painted of her was distorted.
Now she is dead no one can prevent the bright green grass
    from spreading over her grave,
And men weep because of it.

THINKING OF THE FRONTIER
BY LI T'AI-PO

AT what season last year did my Lord leave his Unworthy One?
In the Southern garden, the butterflies were fluttering in the young green grass.
Now, this year, at what season does the Unworthy One cherish thoughts of her Lord?
There is white snow on the Western hills and the clouds of Ch'in are dark.
It is three thousand *li* from here to the Jade Barrier.
I desire to send the " harmonious writings," but how can they reach you?

A SONG OF RESENTMENT
BY LI T'AI-PO

At fifteen, she entered the Palace of Han,
Her flower-face was like a river in Spring.
The Prince chose her of the jade colour
To attend his rest within the embroidered screen.
As she presented the pillow, she was lovely as the evening moon.
He who wears the dragon robes delighted in the sweetly scented wind of her garments.
How was it possible for the "Flying Swallow" to snatch the Emperor's love?
Jealousy unending! Profoundest grief which can so wound a person
And turn the black cloud head-dress to frosted thistledown!

If, for one day, our desires be not satisfied,
Verily the things of the world are nothing.
Change the duck-feather dress for sweet wine,
Cease to embroider dragons on the dresses for the wu dance.
She is chilly with bitterness,
Words cannot be endured.
For one's Lord one plays the table-lute of wu-t'ung wood with strings of silk,

FIR-FLOWER TABLETS

But when one's bowels are torn with grief, the strings also
  break.
Grief in the heart at night is anguish and despair.

PICKING WILLOW
BY LI T'AI-PO

THE drooping willow brushes the very clear water,
Beautifully it flickers in this East-wind time of the year.
Its flowers are bright as the snow of the Jade Pass,
Its leaves soft as smoke against the gold window.
She, the Lovely One, bound in her long thoughts;
Facing them, her heart is burnt with grief.
Pull down a branch,
Gather the Spring colour
And send it far,
Even to that place
Before the Dragon Gate.

AUTUMN RIVER SONG

ON THE BROAD REACH

BY LI T'AI-PO

In the clear green water — the shimmering moon.
In the moonlight — white herons flying.
A young man hears a girl plucking water-chestnuts;
They paddle home together through the night, singing.

VISITING THE TAOIST PRIEST ON THE MOUNTAIN WHICH UPHOLDS HEAVEN. HE IS ABSENT

BY LI T'AI-PO

A DOG,
A dog barking.
And the sound of rushing water.
How dark and rich the peach-flowers after the rain.
Every now and then, between the trees, I see deer.
Twelve o'clock, but I hear no bell in the ravine.
Wild bamboos slit the blue-green of a cloudy sky.
The waterfall hangs against the jade-green peak.
There is no one to tell me where he has gone.
I lean against the pine-trees grieving.

REPLY TO AN UNREFINED PERSON ENCOUNTERED IN THE HILLS

BY LI T'AI-PO

He asks why I perch in the green jade hills.
I smile and do not answer. My heart is comfortable and at peace.
Fallen peach-flowers spread out widely, widely, over the water.
It is another sky and earth, not the world of man.

RECITING VERSES BY MOONLIGHT IN A WESTERN UPPER CHAMBER IN THE CITY OF THE GOLDEN MOUND

BY LI T'AI-PO

The night is still in Chin Ling, a cool wind blows.
I am alone in a high room, gazing over Wu and Yüeh.
White clouds shine on the water and blur the reflection of the still city.
The cold dew soaks my clothes, Autumn moonlight is damp.
In the moonlight, murmuring poems, one loses count of time.
From old days until now, people who can really see with their eyes are few,
Those who understand and speak of a clear river as being bright as silk.
I suggest that men meditate at length on Hsieh Hsüan Hui.

PASSING THE NIGHT AT THE WHITE HERON ISLAND
BY LI T'AI-PO

At dawn, I left the Red Bird Gate;
At sunset, I came to roost on the White Heron Island.
The image of the moon tumbles along the bright surface of the water.
The Tower above the City Gate is lost in the twinkling light of the stars.
I gaze far off, toward my beloved, the Official of Chin Ling,
And the longing in my heart is like that for the Green Jasper Tree.
It is useless to tell my soul to dream;
When it comes back, it will feel the night turned to Autumn.
The green water understands my thoughts,
For me it flows to the Northwest.
Because of this, the sounds of my jade table-lute
Will follow the flowing of its current and carry my grief to my friend.

ASCENDING THE THREE CHASMS
BY LI T'AI-PO

The Sorceress Mountain presses against Green Heaven.
The Serpent River runs terribly fast.
The Serpent River can be suddenly exhausted.
The time may never come when we shall arrive at the Green
      Heaven.
Three dawns shine upon the Yellow Ox.
Three sunsets — and we go so slowly.
Three dawns — again three sunsets —
And we do not notice that our hair is white as silk.

PARTING FROM YANG, A HILL MAN WHO IS RETURNING TO THE HIGH MOUNTAIN
BY LI T'AI-PO

THERE is one place which is an everlasting home to me:
The Jade Woman Peak on the High Southern Mountain.
Often, a wide, flat moonlight
Hangs upon the pines of the whirling Eastern stream.
You are going to pick the fairy grasses
And the shooting purple flower of the *ch'ang p'u*.

After a year, perhaps, you will come to see me
Riding down from the green-blue Heaven on a white dragon.

NIGHT THOUGHTS
BY LI T'AI-PO

In front of my bed the moonlight is very bright.
I wonder if that can be frost on the floor?
I lift up my head and look full at the full moon, the dazzling moon.
I drop my head, and think of the home of old days.

THE SERPENT MOUND
SENT AS A PRESENT TO CHIA THE SECRETARY
BY LI T'AI-PO

CHIA, the Scholar, gazes into the West, thinking of the splendour of the Capitol.
Although you have been transferred to the broad reaches of the river Hsiang, you must not sigh in resentment.
The mercy of the Sainted Lord is far greater than that of Han Wên Ti.
The Princely One had pity, and did not appoint you to the station of the Unending Sands.

ON THE SUBJECT OF OLD TAI'S WINE-SHOP
BY LI T'AI-PO

OLD Tai is gone down to the Yellow Springs.
Yet he must still wish to make " Great Spring Wine."
There is no Li Po on the terrace of Eternal Darkness.
To whom, then, will he sell his wine?

DRINKING IN THE T'AO PAVILION
BY LI T'AI-PO

THE house of the lonely scholar is in the winding lane.
The great scholar's gate is very high.
The garden pool lies and shines like the magic gall mirror;
Groves of trees throw up flowers with wide, open faces;
The leaf-coloured water draws the Spring sun.
Sitting in the green, covered passage-way, watching the
      strange, red clouds of evening,
Listening to the lovely music of flageolets and strings,
The Golden Valley is not much to boast of.

A SONG FOR THE HOUR WHEN THE CROWS ROOST

BY LI T'AI-PO

This is the hour when the crows come to roost on the Ku Su Terrace.
In his Palace, the King of Wu is drinking with Hsi Shih.
Songs of Wu — posturings of Ch'u dances — and yet the revels are not finished.
But already the bright hills hold half of the sun between their lips,
The silver-white arrow-tablet above the gold-coloured brass jar of the water-clock marks the dripping of much water,
And, rising, one can see the Autumn moon sliding beneath the ripples of the river,
While slowly the sun mounts in the East —
What hope for the revels now?

POEM SENT TO THE OFFICIAL WANG OF HAN YANG
BY LI T'AI-PO

The Autumn moon was white upon the Southern Lake.
That night the Official Wang sent me an invitation.
Behind the embroidered bed-curtain lay the Official Secretary
 — drunk.
The woven dresses of the beautiful girls who performed the
 wu dance took charming lines,
The shrill notes of the bamboo flute reached to Mien and O,
The phrases of the songs rose up to the silent clouds.
Now that we are parted, I grieve.
We think of each other a single piece of water distant.

DRINKING ALONE ON THE ROCK IN THE RIVER OF THE CLEAR STREAM
BY LI T'AI-PO

I HAVE a flagon of wine in my hand.
I am alone on the Ancestor Rock in the river.
Since the time when Heaven and Earth were divided,
How many thousand feet has the rock grown?
I lift my cup to Heaven and smile.
Heaven turns round, the sun shines in the West.
I am willing to sit on this rock forever,
Perpetually casting my fish-line like Yen Ling.
Send and ask the man in the midst of the hills
Whether we are not in harmony, both pursuing the same thing.

A FAREWELL BANQUET TO MY FATHER'S YOUNGER BROTHER YÜN, THE IMPERIAL LIBRARIAN

BY LI T'AI-PO

When I was young, I spent the white days lavishly.
I sang — I laughed — I boasted of my ruddy face.
I do not realize that now, suddenly, I am old.
With joy I see the Spring wind return.
It is a pity that we must part, but let us make the best of it and be happy.
We walk to and fro among the peach-trees and plum-trees.
We look at the flowers and drink excellent wine.
We listen to the birds and climb a little way up the bright hills.
Soon evening comes and the bamboo grove is silent.
There is no one — I shut my door.

IN THE PROVINCE OF LU, TO THE EAST OF THE STONE GATE MOUNTAIN, TAKING LEAVE OF TU FU

BY LI T'AI-PO

When drunk, we were divided; but we have been together again for several days.
We have climbed everywhere, to every pool and ledge.
When, on the Stone Gate Road,
Shall we pour from the golden flagon again?
The Autumn leaves drop into the Four Waters,
The Ch'u Mountain is brightly reflected in the colour of the lake.
We are flying like thistledown, each to a different distance;
Pending this, we drain the cups in our hands.

THE MOON OVER THE MOUNTAIN PASS
BY LI T'AI-PO

THE bright moon rises behind the Heaven-high Mountain,
A sea of clouds blows along the pale, wide sky.
The far-off wind has come from nearly ten thousand *li*,
It has blown across the Jade Gate Pass.
Down the Po Têng Road went the people of Han
To waylay the men of Hu beside the Bright Green Bay.
From the beginning, of those who go into battle,
Not one man is seen returning.
The exiled Official gazes at the frontier town,
He thinks of his return home, and his face is very bitter.
Surely to-night, in the distant cupola,
He sighs, and draws heavy breaths. How then can rest be his?

THE TAKING-UP OF ARMS
BY LI T'AI-PO

A HUNDRED battles, the sandy fields of battles, armour broken into fragments.
To the South of the city they are already shut in and surrounded by many layers of men.
They rush out from their cantonments. They shoot and kill the General of the Barbarians.
A single officer leads the routed soldiers of the "Thousand Horsemen" returning whence they came.

A SONG OF THE REST-HOUSE OF DEEP TROUBLE

BY LI T'AI-PO

At Chin Ling, the tavern where travellers part is called the Rest-House of Deep Trouble.

The creeping grass spreads far, far, from the roadside where it started.

There is no end to the ancient sorrow, as water flows to the East.

Grief is in the wind of this place, burning grief in the white aspen.

Like K'ang Lo I climb on board the dull travelling boat.

I hum softly "On the Clear Streams Flies the Night Frost."

It is said that, long ago, on the Ox Island Hill, songs were sung which blended the five colours.

Now do I not equal Hsieh, and the youth of the House of Yüan?

The bitter bamboos make a cold sound, swaying in the Autumn moonlight.

I pass the night alone, desolate behind the reed-blinds, and dream of returning to my distant home.

THE "LOOKING-FOR-HUSBAND" ROCK
BY LI T'AI-PO

In the attitude, and with the manner, of the woman of old,
Full of grief, she stands in the glorious morning light.
The dew is like the tears of to-day;
The mosses like the garments of years ago.
Her resentment is that of the Woman of the Hsiang River;
Her silence that of the concubine of the King of Ch'u.
Still and solitary in the sweet-scented mist,
As if waiting for her husband's return.

AFTER BEING SEPARATED FOR A LONG TIME
BY LI T'AI-PO

How many Springs have we been apart? You do not come
    home.
Five times have I seen the cherry-blossoms from the jade
    window,
Besides there are the "embroidered character letters."
You must sigh as you break the seals.
When this happens, the agony of my longing must stop your
    heart.
I have ceased to wear the cloud head-dress. I have stopped
    combing and dressing the green-black hair on my
    temples.
My sorrow is like a whirling gale — like a flurry of white
    snow.
Last year I sent a letter to the Hill of the Bright Ledge telling
    you these things;
The letter I send this year will again implore you.

East wind — Oh-h-h-h!
East wind, blow for me.
Make the floating cloud come Westward.
I wait his coming, and he does not come.
The fallen flower lies quietly, quietly, thrown upon the green
    moss.

BITTER JEALOUSY IN THE PALACE OF THE HIGH GATE

BY LI T'AI-PO

I

The Heavens have revolved. The "Northern Measure" hangs above the Western wing.
In the Gold House, there is no one; fireflies flit to and fro.
Moonlight seeks to enter the Palace of the High Gate,
To one in the centre of the Palace it brings an added grief.

II

Unending grief in the Cassia Hall. Spring is forgotten.
Autumn dust rises up on the four sides of the Yellow Gold House.
At night, the bright mirror hangs against a dark sky;
It shines upon the solitary one in the Palace of the High Gate.

ETERNALLY THINKING OF EACH OTHER
BY LI T'AI-PO

(The Woman Speaks)

The colour of the day is over; flowers hold the mist in their lips.
The bright moon is like glistening silk. I cannot sleep for grief.
The tones of the Chao psaltery begin and end on the bridge of the silver-crested love-pheasant.
I wish I could play my Shu table-lute on the mandarin duck strings.
The meaning of this music — there is no one to receive it.
I desire my thoughts to follow the Spring wind, even to the Swallow Mountains.
I think of my Lord far, far away, remote as the Green Heaven.
In old days, my eyes were like horizontal waves;
Now they flow, a spring of tears.
If you do not believe that the bowels of your Unworthy One are torn and severed,
Return and take up the bright mirror I was wont to use.

(The Man Speaks)

We think of each other eternally.
My thoughts are at Ch'ang An.

The Autumn cricket chirps beside the railing of the Golden Well;
The light frost is chilly, chilly; the colour of the bamboo sleeping mat is cold.
The neglected lamp does not burn brightly. My thoughts seem broken off.
I roll up the long curtain and look at the moon — it is useless, I sigh continually.
The Beautiful, Flower-like One is as far from me as the distance of the clouds.
Above is the brilliant darkness of a high sky,
Below is the rippling surface of the clear water.
Heaven is far and the road to it is long; it is difficult for a man's soul to compass it in flight.
Even in a dream my spirit cannot cross the grievous barrier of hills.
We think of each other eternally.
My heart and my liver are snapped in two.

PASSIONATE GRIEF

BY LI T'AI-PO

Beautiful is this woman who rolls up the pearl-reed blind.
She sits in an inner chamber,
And her eyebrows, delicate as a moth's antennæ,
Are drawn with grief.
One sees only the wet lines of tears.
For whom does she suffer this misery?
We do not know.

SUNG TO THE AIR: "THE MANTZŬ LIKE AN IDOL"

BY LI T'AI-PO

The trees in the level forest stand in rows and rows,
The mist weaves through them.
The jade-green of the cold hillside country hurts one's heart.
Night colour drifts into the high cupola.
In the cupola, a man grieves.

I stand — stand — on the jade steps, doing nothing.
The birds are flying quickly to roost.
There is the road I should follow if I were going home.
Instead, for me, the " long " rest-houses alternate with the " short " rest-houses.

AT THE YELLOW CRANE TOWER, TAKING LEAVE OF MÊNG HAO JAN ON HIS DEPARTURE TO KUANG LING

BY LI T'AI-PO

I TAKE leave of my dear old friend at the Yellow Crane Tower.
In the flower-smelling mist of the Third Month he will arrive at Yang Chou.
The single sail is shining far off — it is extinguished in the jade-coloured distance,
I see only the long river flowing to the edge of Heaven.

IN DEEP THOUGHT, GAZING AT THE MOON
BY LI T'AI-PO

THE clear spring reflects the thin, wide-spreading pine-tree —
And for how many thousand, thousand years?
No one knows.
The late Autumn moon shivers along the little water ripples,
The brilliance of it flows in through the window.
Before it I sit for a long time absent-mindedly chanting,
Thinking of my friend —
What deep thoughts!
There is no way to see him. How then can we speak together?
Joy is dead. Sorrow is the heart of man.

THOUGHTS FROM A THOUSAND LI
BY LI T'AI-PO

Li Ling is buried in the sands of Hu.
Su Wu has returned to the homes of Han.
Far, far, the Five Spring Pass,
Sorrowful to see the flower-like snow.
He is gone, separated, by a distant country,
But his thoughts return,
Long sighing in grief.
Toward the Northwest
Wild geese are flying.
If I sent a letter — so — to the edge of Heaven.

WORD-PATTERN
BY LI T'AI-PO

The Autumn wind is fresh and clear;
The Autumn moon is bright.
Fallen leaves whirl together and scatter.
The jackdaws, who have gone to roost, are startled again.
We are thinking of each other, but when shall we see each other?
Now, to-night, I suffer, because of my passion.

THE HEAVEN'S GATE MOUNTAINS
BY LI T'AI-PO

In the far distance, the mountains seem to rise out of the river;
Two peaks, standing opposite each other, make a natural
    gateway.
The cold colour of the pines is reflected between the river-banks,
Stones divide the current and shiver the wave-flowers to
    fragments.
Far off, at the border of Heaven, is the uneven line of
    mountain-pinnacles;
Beyond, the bright sky is a blur of rose-tinted clouds.
The sun sets, and the boat goes on and on —
As I turn my head, the mountains sink down into the brilliance
    of the cloud-covered sky.

POEM SENT ON HEARING THAT WANG CH'ANG-LING HAD BEEN EXILED TO LUNG PIAO

BY LI T'AI-PO

In Yang Chou, the blossoms are dropping. The night-jar calls.
I hear it said that you are going to Lung Piao — that you will
    cross the Five Streams.
I fling the grief of my heart up to the bright moon
That it may follow the wind and arrive, straight as eyesight,
    to the West of Yeh Lang.

A PARTING GIFT TO WANG LUN
BY LI T'AI-PO

Li Po gets into a small boat — he is on the point of starting.
Suddenly he hears footsteps on the bank and the sound of
    singing.
The Peach-Flower Pool is a thousand feet deep,
Yet it is not greater than the emotion of Wang Lun as he takes
    leave of me.

SAYING GOOD-BYE TO A FRIEND WHO IS GOING ON AN EXCURSION TO THE PLUM-FLOWER LAKE

BY LI T'AI-PO

I BID you good-bye, my friend, as you are going on an excursion to the Plum-Flower Lake.
You should see the plum-blossoms open;
It is understood that you hire a person to bring me some.
You must not permit the rose-red fragrance to fade.
You will only be at the New Forest Reach a little time,
Since we have agreed to drink at the City of the Golden Mound at full moon.
Nevertheless you must not omit the wild-goose letter,
Or else our knowledge of each other will be as the dust of Hu to the dust of Yüeh.

A POEM SENT TO TU FU FROM SHA CH'IU CH'ÊNG

BY LI T'AI-PO

AFTER all, what have I come here to do?
To lie and meditate at Sha Ch'iu Ch'êng.
Near the city are ancient trees,
And day and night are continuous with Autumn noises.
One cannot get drunk on Lu wine,
The songs of Ch'i have no power to excite emotion.
I think of my friend, and my thoughts are like the Wên River,
Mightily moving, directed toward the South.

BIDDING GOOD-BYE TO YIN SHU
BY LI T'AI-PO

Before the White Heron Island — the moon.
At dawn to-morrow I shall bid good-bye to the returning
    traveller.
The sky is growing bright,
The sun is behind the Green Dragon Hill;
Head high it pushes out of the sea clouds and appears.
Flowing water runs without emotions,
The sail which will carry him away meets the wind and fills.
We watch it together. We cannot bear to be separated.
Again we pledge each other from the cups we hold in our
    hands.

A DESULTORY VISIT TO THE FÊNG HSIEN TEMPLE AT THE DRAGON'S GATE

BY TU FU

I HAD already wandered away from the People's Temple,
But I was obliged to sleep within the temple precincts.
The dark ravine was full of the music of silence,
The moon scattered bright shadows through the forest.
The Great Gate against the sky seemed to impinge upon the paths of the planets.
Sleeping among the clouds, my upper garments, my lower garments, were cold.
Wishing to wake, I heard the sunrise bell
Commanding men to come forth and examine themselves in meditation.

THE THATCHED HOUSE UNROOFED BY AN AUTUMN GALE

BY TU FU

It is the Eighth Month, the very height of Autumn.
The wind rages and roars.
It tears off three layers of my grass-roof.
The thatch flies — it crosses the river — it is scattered about in the open spaces by the river.
High-flying, it hangs, tangled and floating, from the tops of forest trees;
Low-flying, it whirls — turns — and sinks into the hollows of the marsh.
The swarm of small boys from the South Village laugh at me because I am old and feeble.
How dare they act like thieves and robbers before my face,
Openly seizing my thatch and running into my bamboo grove?
My lips are scorched, my mouth dry, I scream at them, but to no purpose.
I return, leaning on my staff. I sigh and breathe heavily.

Presently, of a sudden, the wind ceases. The clouds are the colour of ink.
The Autumn sky is endless — endless — stretching toward dusk and night.

My old cotton quilt is as cold as iron;
My restless son sleeps a troubled sleep, his moving foot tears the quilt.
Over the head of the bed is a leak. Not a place is dry.
The rain streams and stands like hemp — there is no break in its falling.
Since this misery and confusion, I have scarcely slept or dozed.
All the long night, I am soaking wet. When will the light begin to sift in?
If one could have a great house of one thousand, ten thousand rooms —
A great shelter where all the Empire's shivering scholars could have happy faces —
Not moved by wind or rain, solid as a mountain —
Alas! When shall I see that house standing before my eyes?
Then, although my own hut were destroyed, although I might freeze and die, I should be satisfied.

THE RIVER VILLAGE
BY TU FU

The river makes a bend and encircles the village with its current.
All the long Summer, the affairs and occupations of the river village are quiet and simple.
The swallows who nest in the beams go and come as they please.
The gulls in the middle of the river enjoy one another, they crowd together and touch one another.
My old wife paints a chess-board on paper.
My little sons hammer needles to make fish-hooks.
I have many illnesses, therefore my only necessities are medicines;
Besides these, what more can so humble a man as I ask?

THE EXCURSION

A NUMBER OF YOUNG GENTLEMEN OF RANK, ACCOMPANIED BY SINGING-GIRLS, GO OUT TO ENJOY THE COOL OF EVENING. THEY ENCOUNTER A SHOWER OF RAIN

BY TU FU

I

How delightful, at sunset, to loosen the boat!
A light wind is slow to raise waves.
Deep in the bamboo grove, the guests linger;
The lotus-flowers are pure and bright in the cool evening air.
The young nobles stir the ice-water;
The Beautiful Ones wash the lotus-roots, whose fibres are like silk threads.
A layer of clouds above our heads is black.
It will certainly rain, which impels me to write this poem.

II

The rain comes, soaking the mats upon which we are sitting.
A hurrying wind strikes the bow of the boat.
The rose-red rouge of the ladies from Yüeh is wet;
The Yen beauties are anxious about their kingfisher-eyebrows.
We throw out a rope and draw in to the sloping bank. We tie the boat to the willow-trees.

FIR-FLOWER TABLETS

We roll up the curtains and watch the floating wave-flowers.
Our return is different from our setting out. The wind whistles
 and blows in great gusts.
By the time we reach the shore, it seems as though the Fifth
 Month were Autumn.

THE RECRUITING OFFICERS AT THE VILLAGE OF THE STONE MOAT

BY TU FU

I sought a lodging for the night, at sunset, in the Stone Moat Village.
Recruiting Officers, who seize people by night, were there.
A venerable old man climbed over the wall and fled.
An old woman came out of the door and peered.
What rage in the shouts of the Recruiting Officers!
What bitterness in the weeping of the old woman!
I heard the words of the woman as she pled her cause before them:
"My three sons are with the frontier guard at Yeh Ch'êng.
From one son I have received a letter.
A little while ago, two sons died in battle.
He who remains has stolen a temporary lease of life;
The dead are finished forever.
In the house, there is still no grown man,
Only my grandson at the breast.
The mother of my grandson has not gone,
Going out, coming in, she has not a single whole skirt.
I am an old, old woman, and my strength is failing,
But I beg to go with the Recruiting Officers when they return this night.

I will eagerly agree to act as a servant at Ho Yang;
I am still able to prepare the early morning meal."
The sound of words ceased in the long night,
It was as though I heard the darkness choke with tears.
At daybreak, I went on my way,
Only the venerable old man was left.

CROSSING THE FRONTIER
BY TU FU

I

When bows are bent, they should be bent strongly;
When arrows are used, they should be long.
The bow-men should first shoot the horses.
In taking the enemy prisoner, the Leader should first be taken;
There should be no limit to the killing of men.
In making a kingdom, there must naturally be a boundary.
If it were possible to regulate usurpation,
Would so many be killed and wounded?

CROSSING THE FRONTIER
BY TU FU
II

At dawn, the conscripted soldiers enter the camp outside the
    Eastern Gate.
At sunset, they cross the bridge of Ho Yang.
The setting sunlight is reflected on the great flags.
Horses neigh. The wind whines — whines —
Ten thousand tents are spread along the level sand.
Officers instruct their companies.
The bright moon hangs in the middle of the sky.
The written orders are strict that the night shall be still and
    empty.
Sadness everywhere. A few sounds from a Mongol flageolet
    jar the air.
The strong soldiers are no longer proud, they quiver with
    sadness.
May one ask who is their General?
Perhaps it is Ho P'iao Yao.

THE SORCERESS GORGE
BY TU FU

Jade dew lies upon the withered and wounded forest of maple-trees.

On the Sorceress Hill, over the Sorceress Gorge, the mist is desolate and dark.

The ripples of the river increase into waves and blur with the rapidly flowing sky.

The wind-clouds at the horizon become confused with the Earth. Darkness.

The myriad chrysanthemums have bloomed twice. Days to come — tears.

The solitary little boat is moored, but my heart is in the old-time garden.

Everywhere people are hastening to measure and cut out their Winter clothes.

At sunset, in the high City of the White Emperor, the hurried pounding of washed garments.

THINKING OF LI PO ON A SPRING DAY
BY TU FU

THE poems of Po are unequalled.
His thoughts are never categorical, but fly high in the wind.
His poems are clear and fresh as those of Yü, the official;
They are fine and easy as those of Pao, the military counsellor.
I am North of the river Wei, looking at the Spring trees;
You are East of the river, watching the sunset clouds.
When shall we meet over a jug of wine?
When shall I have another precious discussion of literature
  with you?

AT THE EDGE OF HEAVEN. THINKING OF LI T'AI-PO
BY TU FU

A COLD wind blows up from the edge of Heaven.
The state of mind of the superior man is what?
When does the wild goose arrive?
Autumn water flows high in the rivers and lakes.

They hated your essay — yet your fate was to succeed.
The demons where you are rejoice to see men go by.
You should hold speech with the soul of Yüan,
And toss a poem into the Mi Lo River as a gift to him.

SENT TO LI PO AS A GIFT
BY TU FU

Autumn comes,
We meet each other.
You still whirl about as a thistledown in the wind.
Your Elixir of Immortality is not yet perfected
And, remembering Ko Hung, you are ashamed.
You drink a great deal,
You sing wild songs,
Your days pass in emptiness.
Your nature is a spreading fire,
It is swift and strenuous.
But what does all this bravery amount to?

A TOAST FOR MÊNG YÜN-CH'ING
BY TU FU

ILLIMITABLE happiness,
But grief for our white heads.
We love the long watches of the night, the red candle.
It would be difficult to have too much of meeting,
Let us not be in a hurry to talk of separation.
But because the Heaven River will sink,
We had better empty the wine-cups.
To-morrow, at bright dawn, the world's business will entangle
 us.
We brush away our tears,
We go — East and West.

MOON NIGHT
BY TU FU

To-night — the moon at Fu Chou.
In the centre of the Women's Apartments
There is only one to look at it.
I am far away, but I love my little son, my daughter.
They cannot understand and think of Ch'ang An.
The sweet-smelling mist makes the cloud head-dress damp,
The jade arm must be chilly
In this clear, glorious shining.
When shall I lean on the lonely screen?
When shall we both be shone upon, and the scars of tears be dry?

HEARING THE EARLY ORIOLE (WRITTEN IN EXILE)

BY PO CHÜ-I

THE sun rose while I slept. I had not yet risen
When I heard an early oriole above the roof of my house.
Suddenly it was like the Royal Park at dawn,
With birds calling from the branches of the ten-thousand-year trees.
I thought of my time as a Court Official
When I was meticulous with my pencil in the Audience Hall.
At the height of Spring, in occasional moments of leisure,
I would look at the grass and growing things,
And at dawn and at dusk I would hear this sound.
Where do I hear it now?
In the lonely solitude of the City of Hsün Yang.
The bird's song is certainly the same,
The change is in the emotions of the man.
If I could only stop thinking that I am at the ends of the earth,
I wonder, would it be so different from the Palace after all?

THE CITY OF STONES. (NANKING)
BY LIU YÜ-HSI

HILLS surround the ancient kingdom; they never change.
The tide beats against the empty city, and silently, silently, returns.
To the East, over the Huai River — the ancient moon.
Through the long, quiet night it moves, crossing the battlemented wall.

SUNG TO THE TUNE OF "THE UNRIPE HAWTHORN BERRY"

BY NIU HSI-CHI

Mist is trying to hide the Spring-coloured hills,
The sky is pale, the stars are scattered and few.
The moon is broken and fading, yet there is light on your face,
These are the tears of separation, for now it is bright dawn.

We have said many words,
But our passion is not assuaged.
Turn your head, I have still something to say:
Remember my skirt of green open-work silk,
The sweet-scented grasses everywhere will prevent your forgetting.

WRITTEN BY WANG WEI, IN THE MANNER OF CHIA, THE (PALACE) SECRETARY, AFTER AN IMPERIAL AUDIENCE AT DAWN IN THE "PALACE OF GREAT BRILLIANCE"

At the first light of the still-concealed sun, the Cock-man, in his dark-red cap, strikes the tally-sticks and proclaims aloud the hour.

At this exact moment, the Keeper of the Robes sends in the eider-duck skin dress, with its cloud-like curving feather-scales of kingfisher green.

In the Ninth Heaven, the Ch'ang Ho Gate opens; so do those of the Palaces, and the Halls of Ceremony in the Palaces.

The ten thousand kingdoms send their ambassadors in the dresses and caps of their ranks to do reverence before the pearl-stringed head-dress.

The immediately-arrived sun tips the "Immortal Palm"; it glitters.

Sweet-scented smoke rises and flows about the Emperor's ceremonial robes, making the dragons writhe.

The audience ended, I wish to cut the paper of five colours and write upon it the words of the Son of Heaven.

My jade girdle-ornaments clash sweetly as I return to sit beside the Pool of the Crested Love-Pheasant.

THE BLUE-GREEN STREAM
BY WANG WEI

EVERY time I have started for the Yellow Flower River,
I have gone down the Blue-Green Stream,
Following the hills, making ten thousand turnings.
We go along rapidly, but advance scarcely one hundred *li*.
We are in the midst of a noise of water,
Of the confused and mingled sounds of water broken by stones,
And in the deep darkness of pine-trees.
Rocked, rocked,
Moving on and on,
We float past water-chestnuts
Into a still clearness reflecting reeds and rushes.
My heart is clean and white as silk; it has already achieved
      Peace;
It is smooth as the placid river.
I long to stay here, curled up on the rocks,
Dropping my fish-line forever.

FARM HOUSE ON THE WEI STREAM
BY WANG WEI

The slanting sun shines on the cluster of small houses upon the heights.
Oxen and sheep are coming home along the distant lane.
An old countryman is thinking of the herd-boy,
He leans on his staff by the thorn-branch gate, watching.
Pheasants are calling, the wheat is coming into ear,
Silk-worms sleep, the mulberry-leaves are thin.
Labourers, with their hoes over their shoulders, arrive;
They speak pleasantly together, loth to part.
It is for this I long — unambitious peace!
Disappointed in my hopes, dissatisfied, I hum "Dwindled and Shrunken."

SEEKING FOR THE HERMIT OF THE WEST HILL; NOT MEETING HIM
BY CH'IU WEI

On the Nothing-Beyond Peak, a hut of red grass.
I mount straight up for thirty *li*.
I knock at the closed door — no serving boy.
I look into the room. There is only the low table, and the
    stand for the elbows.
If you are not sitting on the cloth seat of your rough wood
    cart,
Then you must be fishing in the Autumn water.
We have missed each other; we have not seen each other;
My effort to do you homage has been in vain.
The grass is the colour which rain leaves.
From inside the window, I hear the sound of pine-trees at dusk.
There is no greater solitude than to be here.
My ears hear it; my heart spreads open to it naturally.
Although I lack the entertainment of a host,
I have received much — the whole doctrine of clear purity.
My joy exhausted, I descend the hill.
Why should I wait for the Man of Wisdom?

FLOATING ON THE POOL OF JO YA. SPRING
BY CHI WU-CH'IEN

SOLITARY meditation is not suddenly snapped off; it continues without interruption.
It flows — drifts this way, that way — returns upon itself.
The boat moves before a twilight wind.
We enter the mouth of the pool by the flower path
At the moment when night enfolds the Western Valley.
The serrated hills face the Southern Constellation,
Mist hangs over the deep river pools and floats down gently, gently, with the current.
Behind me, through the trees, the moon is sinking.
The business of the world is a swiftly moving space of water, a rushing, spreading water.
I am content to be an old man holding a bamboo fishing-rod.

SUNG TO THE AIR: "THE WANDERER"
(COMPOSED BY SU WU IN THE TIME OF THE EMPEROR WU OF HAN)
BY MÊNG CHIAO

THREAD from the hands of a doting mother
Worked into the clothes of a far-off journeying son.
Before his departure, were the close, fine stitches set,
Lest haply his return be long delayed.
The heart — the inch-long grass —
Who will contend that either can repay
The gentle brightness of the Third Month of Spring.

FAREWELL WORDS TO THE DAUGHTER OF THE HOUSE OF YANG
BY WEI YING-WU

BECAUSE of this, sad, sad has the whole day been to me.
You must go forth and journey, far, very far.
The time has come when you, the maiden, must go.
The light boat ascends the great river.
Your particular bitterness is to have none from whom you may claim support.
I have cherished you. I have pondered over you. I have been increasingly gentle and tender to you.
A child taken from those who have cared for it —
On both sides separation brings the tears which will not cease.
Facing this, the very centre of the bowels is knotted.
It is your duty, you must go. It is scarcely possible to delay farther.
From early childhood, you have lacked a mother's guidance,
How then will you know to serve your husband's mother? I am anxious.
From this time, the support on which you must rely is the home of your husband.
You will find kindness and sympathy, therefore you must not grumble;
Modesty and thrift are indeed to be esteemed.

Money and jewels, maid-servants and furnishings — are these necessary, a perfection to be waited for?
The way of a wife should be filial piety, respect and compliance;
Your manner, your conduct, should be in accord with this way.
To-day, at dawn, we part.
How many Autumns will pass before I see you?
Usually I endeavour to command my feelings,
But now, when my emotions come upon me suddenly, they are difficult to control.
Being returned home, I look at my own little girl.
My tears fall as rain. They trickle down the string of my cap and continue to flow.

SUNG TO THE AIR: "LOOKING SOUTH OVER THE RIVER AND DREAMING"
BY WÊN T'ING-YÜN

The hair is combed,
The face is washed,
All is done.

Alone, in the upper story of my Summer-house, I bend forward,
　　　looking at the river.
A thousand sails pass — but among all of them the one is not.
The slant sunlight will not speak,
It will not speak.
The long-stretched water scarcely moves.

My bowels are broken within me.
Oh! Island of the White Water Flowers!

TOGETHER WE KNOW HAPPINESS
WRITTEN BY A DESCENDANT OF THE FOUNDER OF THE SOUTHERN T'ANG DYNASTY

SILENT and alone, I ascended the West Cupola.
The moon was like a golden hook.
In the quiet, empty, inner courtyard, the coolness of early Autumn enveloped the wu-t'ung tree.

Scissors cannot cut this thing;
Unravelled, it joins again and clings.
It is the sorrow of separation,
And none other tastes to the heart like this.

ONCE MORE FIELDS AND GARDENS
BY T'AO YÜAN-MING

Even as a young man
I was out of tune with ordinary pleasures.
It was my nature to love the rooted hills,
The high hills which look upon the four edges of Heaven.
What folly to spend one's life like a dropped leaf
Snared under the dust of streets,
But for thirteen years it was so I lived.

The caged bird longs for the fluttering of high leaves.
The fish in the garden pool languishes for the whirled water
Of meeting streams.
So I desired to clear and seed a patch of the wild Southern
    moor.
And always a countryman at heart,
I have come back to the square enclosures of my fields
And to my walled garden with its quiet paths.

Mine is a little property of ten *mou* or so,
A thatched house of eight or nine rooms.
On the North side, the eaves are overhung
With the thick leaves of elm-trees,
And willow-trees break the strong force of the wind.

FIR-FLOWER TABLETS

On the South, in front of the great hall,
Peach-trees and plum-trees spread a net of branches
Before the distant view.

The village is hazy, hazy,
And mist sucks over the open moor.
A dog barks in the sunken lane which runs through the village.
A cock crows, perched on a clipped mulberry.

There is no dust or clatter
In the courtyard before my house.
My private rooms are quiet,
And calm with the leisure of moonlight through an open door.

For a long time I lived in a cage;
Now I have returned.
For one must return
To fulfil one's nature.

SONG OF THE SNAPPED WILLOW
WRITTEN DURING THE LIANG DYNASTY

When he mounted his horse, he did not take his leather riding-
    whip;
He pulled down and snapped off the branch of a willow-tree.
When he dismounted, he blew into his horizontal flute,
And it was as though the fierce grief of his departure would
    destroy the traveller.

THE CLOUDY RIVER

(FROM THE "BOOK OF ODES")

How the Cloudy River glitters —
Shining, revolving in the sky!
The King spoke:
"Alas! Alas!
What crime have the men of to-day committed
That Heaven sends down upon them
Confusion and death?
The grain does not sprout,
The green harvests wither,
Again and again this happens.
There is no spirit to whom I have not rendered homage,
No sacrifice I have withheld for love.
My stone sceptres and round badges of rank have come to an
    end.
Why have I not been heard?

Already the drought is terrible beyond expression!
The heated air is overpowering; it is a concentrated fierceness.
I have not ceased to offer the pure sacrifices,
I myself have gone from the border altars to the ancestral
    temples.
To Heaven,
To Earth,

FIR-FLOWER TABLETS

I have made the proper offerings,
I have buried them in the ground.
There is no spirit I have not honoured,
Hou Chi could do no more.
Shang Ti does not look favourably upon us.
This waste and ruin of the Earth —
If my body alone might endure it!

Already the drought is terrible beyond expression!
I cannot evade the responsibility of it.
I am afraid — afraid; I feel in peril — I feel in peril,
As when one hears the clap of thunder and the roll of thunder.
Of the remnant of the black-haired people of Chou
There will not be left so much as half a man.
Ruler over the high, wide Heavens,
Even I shall not be spared.
Why should I not be terrified
Since the ancestral sacrifices will be ended?

Already the drought is terrible beyond expression!
The consequences of it cannot be prevented.
Scorching — scorching!
Blazing — blazing!
No living place is left to me.
The Great Decree of Fate is near its end.
There is none to look up to; none whose counsel I might ask.
The many great officials, the upright men of ancient days,

Cannot advise me in regard to these consequences.
My father, my mother, my remote ancestors,
How can you endure this which has befallen me?

Already the drought is terrible beyond expression!
Parched and scoured the hills, the streams.
Drought, the Demon of Drought, has caused these ravages,
Like a burning fire which consumes everything.
My heart is shrivelled with the heat;
Sorrow rises from the heart as smoke from fire.
The many great officials, the upright men of ancient days,
Do not listen to me.
Ruler of the high, wide Heavens,
Permit that I retire to obscurity.

Already the drought is terrible beyond expression!
I strive, and force myself in vain.
I dread that which will come.
How — why — should I bear this madness of drought?
I suffer not to know the reason for it.
I offered the yearly sacrifices for full crops in good time.
I neglected not one of the Spirits of the Four Quarters of the Earth.
The Ruler of the high, wide Heavens
Does not even consider me.
I have worshipped and reverenced the bright gods,
They should not be dissatisfied or angry with me.

Already the drought is terrible beyond expression!
Everything is in confusion; all authority is gone;
My officials are reduced to extremity.
My Chief Minister is afflicted with a continuing illness.
My Master of the Horse, my Commander of the Guards,
My Steward, my attendants of the Right and of the Left,
Not one among them has failed to try and help the people,
Not one has given up because powerless.
I raise my head and look at the Ruler of the wide, bright
    Heavens.
I cry: 'Why must I suffer such grief!'

I look upwards. I gaze at the wide, bright Heavens,
There are little stars twinkling, even those stars.
My officers and the great men of my country,
You have wrought sincerely and without gain.
The Great Decree is near its end.
Do not abandon what you have partly accomplished,
Your prayers are not for me alone,
But to guard the people and those who watch over them from
    calamity.
I look upwards. I gaze at the wide, bright Heavens.
When shall I receive the favour of rest?"

TO THE AIR: "THE FALLEN LEAVES AND THE PLAINTIVE CICADA"
BY THE EMPEROR WU OF HAN

There is no rustle of silken sleeves,
Dust gathers in the Jade Courtyard.
The empty houses are cold, still, without sound.
The leaves fall and lie upon the bars of doorway after doorway.
I long for the Most Beautiful One; how can I attain my desire?
Pain bursts my heart. There is no peace.

WRITTEN IN EARLY AUTUMN AT THE POOL OF SPRINKLING WATER

BY CHAO TI OF HAN, THE "BRIGHT EMPEROR"

In Autumn, when the landscape is clear, to float over the wide, water ripples,
To pick the water-chestnut and the lotus-flower with a quick, light hand!
The fresh wind is cool, we start singing to the movement of the oars.
The clouds are bright; they part before the light of dawn; the moon has sunk below the Silver River.
Enjoying such pleasure for ten thousand years —
Could one consider it too much?

PROCLAIMING THE JOY OF CERTAIN HOURS
BY THE EMPEROR LING OF (LATER) HAN

Cool wind rising. Sun sparkling on the wide canal.
Pink lotuses, bent down by day, spread open at night.
There is too much pleasure; a day cannot contain it.
Clear sounds of strings, smooth flowing notes of flageolets —
　　we sing the " Jade Love-Bird " song.
A thousand years? Ten thousand? Nothing could exceed such
　　delight.

A SONG OF GRIEF

BY PAN CHIEH-YÜ

Glazed silk, newly cut, smooth, glittering, white,
As white, as clear, even as frost and snow.
Perfectly fashioned into a fan,
Round, round, like the brilliant moon,
Treasured in my Lord's sleeve, taken out, put in —
Wave it, shake it, and a little wind flies from it.
How often I fear the Autumn Season's coming
And the fierce, cold wind which scatters the blazing heat.
Discarded, passed by, laid in a box alone;
Such a little time, and the thing of love cast off.

A LETTER OF THANKS FOR PRECIOUS PEARLS BESTOWED BY ONE ABOVE

BY CHIANG TS'AI-P'IN

(THE "PLUM-BLOSSOM" CONCUBINE OF THE EMPEROR MING HUANG)

It is long — long — since my two eyebrows were painted like cassia-leaves.
I have ended the adorning of myself. My tears soak my dress of coarse red silk.
All day I sit in the Palace of the High Gate. I do not wash; I do not comb my hair.
How can precious pearls soothe so desolate a grief.

DANCING
BY YANG KUEI-FEI
(THE "WHITE POPLAR" IMPERIAL CONCUBINE OF
THE EMPEROR MING HUANG)

Wide sleeves sway.
Scents,
Sweet scents
Incessantly coming.

It is red lilies,
Lotus lilies,
Floating up,
And up,
Out of Autumn mist.

Thin clouds
Puffed,
Fluttered,
Blown on a rippling wind
Through a mountain pass.

Young willow shoots
Touching,
Brushing,
The water
Of the garden pool.

SONGS OF THE COURTESANS
(WRITTEN DURING THE LIANG DYNASTY)
ONE OF THE "SONGS OF THE TEN REQUESTS"
BY TING LIU NIANG

My skirt is cut out of peacock silk,
Red and green shine together, they are also opposed.
It dazzles like the gold-chequered skin of the scaly dragon.
Clearly so odd and lovely a thing must be admired.
My Lord himself knows well the size.
I beg thee, my Lover, give me a girdle.

AI AI THINKS OF THE MAN SHE LOVES

How often must I pass the moonlight nights alone?
I gaze far — far — for the Seven Scents Chariot.
My girdle drops because my waist is shrunken.
The golden hairpins of my disordered head-dress are all askew.

SENT TO HER LOVER YÜAN AT HO NAN (SOUTH OF THE RIVER) BY CHANG PI LAN (JADE-GREEN ORCHID) FROM HU PEI (NORTH OF THE LAKE)

My Lover is like the tree-peony of Lo Yang.
I, unworthy, like the common willows of Wu Ch'ang.
Both places love the Spring wind.
When shall we hold each other's hands again?

CH'IN, THE "FIRE-BIRD WITH PLUMAGE WHITE AS JADE," LONGS FOR HER LOVER

Incessant the buzzing of insects beyond the orchid curtain.
The moon flings slanting shadows from the pepper-trees
    across the courtyard.
Pity the girl of the flowery house,
Who is not equal to the blossoms
Of Lo Yang.

THE GREAT HO RIVER
BY THE MOTHER OF THE LORD OF SUNG
(FROM "THE BOOK OF ODES")

Who says the Ho is wide?
Why one little reed can bridge it.

Who says that Sung is far?
I stand on tiptoe and see it.

Who says the Ho is wide?
Why the smallest boat cannot enter.

Who says that Sung is far?
It takes not a morning to reach it

WRITTEN PICTURES

AN EVENING MEETING

The night is the colour of Spring mists.
The lamp-flower falls,
And the flame bursts out brightly.
In the midst of the disorder of the dressing-table
Lies a black eye-stone.
As she dances,
A golden hairpin drops to the ground.
She peeps over her fan,
Arch, coquettish, welcoming his arrival.
Then suddenly striking the strings of her table-lute,
She sings —
But what is the rain of the Sorceress Gorge
Doing by the shore of the Western Sea?

Li Hai-ku, 19th Century

THE EMPEROR'S RETURN FROM A JOURNEY
TO THE SOUTH

Like a saint, he comes,
The Most Noble.
In his lacquered state chariot
He awes the hundred living things.
He is clouded with the purple smoke of incense,
A round umbrella
Protects the Son of Heaven.
Exquisite is the beauty
Of the two-edged swords,
Of the chariots,
Of the star-embroidered shoes of the attendants.
The Sun and Moon fans are borne before him,
And he is preceded by sharp spears
And the blowing brightness of innumerable flags.
The Spring wind proclaims the Emperor's return,
Binding the ten thousand districts together
In a chorded harmony of Peace and Satisfaction,
So that the white-haired old men and the multitudes rejoice,
And I wish to add my ode
In praise of perfect peace.
                    Wên Chêng-ming, 16th Century

ON SEEING THE PORTRAIT OF A BEAUTIFUL CONCUBINE

Fine rain,
Spring mud
Slippery as bean curds.
In a rose-red flash, she approaches —
Beautiful, sparkling like wine;
Tottering as though overcome with wine.
Her little feet slip on the sliding path;
Who will support her?
Clearly it is her picture
We see here,
In a rose-red silken dress,
Her hair plaited like the folds
Of the hundred clouds.
It is Manshu.

CH'EN HUNG-SHOU, 19th Century

CALLIGRAPHY

The writing of Li Po-hai
Is like the vermilion bird
And the blue-green dragon.
It drifts slowly as clouds drift;
It has the wide swiftness of wind.
Hidden within it lurk the dragon and the tiger.

The writing of Chia, the official,
Is like the high hat of ceremonial.
It flashes like flowers in the hair,
And its music is the trailing of robes
And the sweet tinkling of jade girdle-pendants.
Because of his distinguished position,
He never says anything not sanctioned by precedent.
      Liang T'ung-shu, 18th Century

THE PALACE BLOSSOMS

When the rain ceases,
The white water flowers of Ch'ang Lo stroll together at sunset
In the City by the River.
The young girls are no longer confined
In the gold pavilions,
But may gaze at the green water
Whirling under the bridge of many turnings.

Tai Ta-mien, 18th Century

ONE GOES A JOURNEY

He is going to the Tung T'ing Lake,
My friend whom I have loved so many years.
The Spring wind startles the willows
And they break into pale leaf.
I go with my friend
As far as the river-bank.
He is gone —
And my mind is filled and overflowing
With the things I did not say.

Again the white water flower
Is ripe for plucking.
The green, pointed swords of the iris
Splinter the brown earth.
To the South of the river
Are many sweet-olive trees.
I gather branches of them to give to my friend
On his return.

      Liu Shih-an, 18th Century

FROM THE STRAW HUT AMONG THE SEVEN PEAKS

I

From the high pavilion of the great rock,
I look down at the green river.
There is the sail of a returning boat.
The birds are flying in pairs.
The faint snuff colour of trees
Closes the horizon.
All about me
Sharp peaks jag upward;
But through my window,
And beyond,
Is the smooth, broad brightness
Of the setting sun.

II

Clouds brush the rocky ledge.
In the dark green shadow left by the sunken sun
A jade fountain flies,
And a little stream,
Thin as the fine thread spun by sad women in prison chambers,
Slides through the grasses
And whirls suddenly upon itself

FIR-FLOWER TABLETS

Avoiding the sharp edges of the iris-leaves.
Few people pass here.
Only the hermits of the hills come in companies
To gather the Imperial Fern.

Lu Kun, 19th Century

ON THE CLASSIC OF THE HILLS AND SEA

In what place does the cinnabar-red tree of the alchemists
    seed?
Upon the sun-slopes
Of Mount Mi
It pushes out its yellow flowers
And rounds its crimson fruit.
Eat it and you will live forever.

The frozen dew is like white jade;
It shimmers with the curious light of gems.

Why do people regard these things?
Because the Yellow Emperor considers them of importance.

                Written by LI HAI-KU, 19th Century
    Composed by T'AO CH'IEN

THE HERMIT

A COLD rain blurs the edges of the river.
Night enters Wu.
In the level brightness of dawn
I saw my friend start alone for the Ch'u Mountain.
He gave me this message for his friends and relations at Lo
      Yang:
My heart is a piece of ice in a jade cup.
                    Written by LI HAI-KU, 19th Century
  Composed by WANG CH'ANG-LING

AFTER HOW MANY YEARS
SPRING

The willows near the roadside rest-house are soft with new-burst buds.
I saunter along the river path,
Listening to the occasional beating of the ferry drum.
Clouds blow and separate,
And between them I see the watch towers
Of the distant city.
They come in official coats
To examine my books.
Months go by;
Years slide backwards and disappear.
Musing,
I shut my eyes
And think of the road I have come,
And of the Spring weeds
Choking the fields of my house.

SUMMER

The rain has stopped.
The clouds drive in a new direction.
The sand is so dry and hard that my wooden shoes ring upon it
As I walk.

FIR-FLOWER TABLETS

The flowers in the wind are very beautiful.
A little stream quietly draws a line
Through the sand.
Every household is drunk with sacrificial wine,
And every field is tall with millet
And pale young wheat.
I have not much business.
It is a good day.
I smile.
I will write a poem
On all this sudden brightness.

AUTUMN

Hoar-frost is falling,
And the water of the river runs clear.
The moon has not yet risen,
But there are many stars.
I hear the watch-dogs
In the near-by village.
On the opposite bank
Autumn lamps are burning in the windows.
I am sick,
Sick with all the illnesses there are.
I can bear this cold no longer,
And a great pity for my whole past life
Fills my mind.
The boat has started at last.

FIR-FLOWER TABLETS

O be careful not to run foul
Of the fishing-nets!

WINTER

I was lonely in the cold valleys
Where I was stationed.
But I am still lonely,
And when no one is near
I sigh.
My gluttonous wife rails at me
To guard her bamboo shoots.
My son is ill and neglects to water
The flowers.
Oh yes,
Old red rice can satisfy hunger,
And poor people can buy muddy, unstrained wine
On credit.
But the pile of land-tax bills
Is growing;
I will go over and see my neighbour,
Leaning on my staff.

      Li Hai-ku, 19th Century

THE INN AT THE MOUNTAIN PASS

I RETURN to the inn at the foot of the Climbing Bean Pass.
The smooth skin of the water shines,
And the clouds slip over the sky.
This is the twilight of dawn and dusk.
On the top of Hsi Lêng
The hill priest sits in the evening
And meditates.
Two —
Two —
Those are the lights of fishing-boats
Arriving at the door.

      WANG CHING-TS'ÊNG, 19th Century

LI T'AI-PO MEDITATES

Li Po climbed the Flowery Mountain
As far as the Peak of the Fallen Precipice.
Gazing upward, he said:
" From this little space my breath can reach the God Star."
He sighed, regretting his irresolution, and thought:
" Hsieh T'iao alarms people with his poetry.
I can only scratch my head
And beseech the Green Heaven
To regard me."

       Ho Ping-shou, 19th Century

PAIR OF SCROLLS

Shoals of fish assemble and scatter,
Suddenly there is no trace of them.

The single butterfly comes—
Goes—
Comes—
Returning as though urged by love.

Ho Shao-chi, 19th Century

TWO PANELS

By the scent of the burning pine-cones,
I read the "Book of Changes."

Shaking the dew from the lotus-flowers,
I write T'ang poetry.

LIANG T'UNG-SHU, 19th Century

THE RETURN

He is a solitary traveller
Returning to his home in the West.
Ah, but how difficult to find the way!
He has journeyed three thousand *li*.
He has attended an Imperial audience at the Twelve Towers.
He sees the slanting willows by the road
With their new leaves,
But when he left his house
His eyes were dazzled by the colours
Of Autumn.
What darkness fills them now!
He is far from the Autumn-bright hills
He remembers.
The spread of the river before him is empty,
It slides — slides.

Li Hai-ku, 19th Century

EVENING CALM

The sun has set.
The sand sparkles.
The sky is bright with afterglow.
The small waves flicker,
And the swirling water rustles the stones.
In the white path of the moon,
A small boat drifts,
Seeking for the entrance
To the stream of many turnings.
Probably there is snow
On the shady slopes of the hills.

      Kao Shih-chi, 19th Century

FISHING PICTURE

The fishermen draw their nets
From the great pool of the T'an River.
They have hired a boat
And come here to fish by the reflected light
Of the sunken sun.
          Ta Chung-kuang, 19th Century

FACSIMILE OF ORIGINAL "HANGING-ON-THE-WALL POEM" ENTITLED "FISHING PICTURE"

SPRING. SUMMER. AUTUMN

The stream at the foot of the mountain
Runs all day.
Even far back in the hills,
The grass is growing;
Spring is late there.
From all about comes the sound
Of dogs barking
And chickens cheeping.
They are stripping the mulberry-trees,
But who planted them?

What a wind!
We start in our boat
To gather the red water-chestnut.
Leaning on my staff,
I watch the sun sink
Behind the Western village.
I can see the apricot-trees
Set on their raised stone platform,
With an old fisherman standing
Beside them.
It makes me think
Of the Peach-Blossom Fountain,

FIR-FLOWER TABLETS

And the houses
Clustered about it.

Let us meet beside the spring
And drink wine together.
I will bring my table-lute;
It is good
To lean against
The great pines.
In the gardens to the South,
The sun-flowers are wet with dew;
They will pick them at dawn.
And all night
In the Western villages
One hears the sound of yellow millet being pounded.

Li Hai-ku, 19th Century

NOTES

NOTES

SONGS OF THE MARCHES

Note 1. *It is the Fifth Month,*
But still the Heaven-high hills
Shine with snow.

  The Fifth Month corresponds to June. (See Introduction.) The Heaven-high hills are the T'ien Shan Mountains, which run across the Northern part of Central Asia and in places attain a height of 20,000 feet. (See map.)

Note 2. *Playing "The Snapped Willow."*

  The name of an old song suggesting homesickness; it is translated in this volume. It was written during the Liang Dynasty (A.D. 502–557). References to it are very common in Chinese poetry.

Note 3. *So that they may be able in an instant to rush upon the Barbarians.*

  The Chinese regarded the tribes of Central Asia, known by the generic name of Hsiung Nu, as Barbarians, and often spoke of them as such. It was during the reign of Shih Huang Ti (221–206 B.C.) that these tribes first seriously threatened China, and it was to resist their incursions that the Great Wall was built. They were a nomadic people, moving from place to place in search of fresh pasture for their herds. They were famous for their horsemanship and always fought on horseback.

Note 4. *And the portrait of Ho P'iao Yao*
Hangs magnificently in the Lin Pavilion.

  Ho P'iao Yao was a famous leader whose surname was

NOTES

Ho. He was given the pseudonym of P'iao Yao, meaning "to whirl with great speed to the extreme limit," because of his energy in fighting. His lust for war was so terrible that the soldiers under him always expected to be killed. After his death, the Emperor Wu of Han erected a tomb in his honour. It was covered with blocks of stone in order that it might resemble the Ch'i Lien Mountains, where Ho P'iao Yao's most successful battles had been fought.

The Lin Pavilion was a Hall where the portraits of distinguished men were hung.

Note 5. The Heavenly soldiers arise.

The Chinese soldiers were called the "Heavenly Soldiers" because they fought for the Emperor, who was the Son of Heaven.

Note 6. Divides the tiger tally.

A disk broken in half, worn as a proof of identity and authority. The General was given one half, the Emperor kept the other.

Note 7. The Jade Pass has not yet been forced.

In order to reach the Central Asian battle-fields, the soldiers were obliged to go out through the Jade Pass, or Barrier, which lay in the curious bottle-neck of land between the mountain ranges which occupy the centre of the continent. (See map.)

Note 8. They seized the snow of the Inland Sea.

The Inland, or Green Sea, is the Chinese name for the Kokonor Lake lying West of the Kansu border. (See map.)

Note 9. They lay on the sand at the top of the Dragon Mound.

The Dragon Mound is a high ridge of land on the Western border of Shensi, now comprising part of the Eastern

NOTES

boundary of Kansu. The native accounts say that the road encircles the mountains nine times, and that it takes seven days to make the ascent. "Its height is not known. From its summit, one can see five hundred *li*. To the East, lie the homes of men; to the West, wild wastes. The sound of a stone thrown over the precipice is heard for several *li*."

Note 10. All this they bore that the Moon Clan.

Name of one of the Hsiung Nu tribes. It was this tribe, known to Europeans under name of Huns, who overran Europe in the Fifth Century.

THE PERILS OF THE SHU ROAD

Note 11. During the reign of the T'ang Emperor, Hsüan Tsung (A.D. 712–756), better known as Ming Huang, a rebellion broke out under An Lu-shan, an official who had for many years enjoyed the Emperor's supreme favour. Opinions among the advisers to the throne differed as to whether or not the Emperor had better fly from his capital and take refuge in the province of Szechwan, the ancient Shu. Li T'ai-po strongly disapproved of the step, but as he was no longer in office could only express his opinion under the guise of a poem. This poem, which the Chinese read in a metaphorical sense, describes the actual perils of the road leading across the Mountains of the Two-Edged Sword, the only thoroughfare into Szechwan. Li T'ai-po's counsel did not prevail, however, and the Emperor did actually flee, but not until after the poem was written.

Note 12. No greater undertaking than this has been since Ts'an Ts'ung and Yü Fu ruled the land.

These were early Rulers. Ts'an Ts'ung was the first

NOTES

King of Shu, the modern Szechwan. He was supposed to be a descendant of the semi-legendary Yellow Emperor.

Note 13. But the earth of the mountain fell and overwhelmed the Heroes so that they perished.

An historical allusion to five strong men sent by the King of Shu to obtain the daughters of the King of Ch'in.

Note 14. Above, the soaring tips of the high mountains hold back the six dragons of the sun.

The sun is supposed to drive round the Heavens once every day in a chariot drawn by six dragons and driven by a charioteer named Hsi Ho.

Note 15. The gibbons climb and climb.

Gibbons, which are very common in this part of China, are a small species of tailless ape, thoroughly arboreal in their habits. They make the woods sound with unearthly cries at night, and are unsurpassed in agility and so swift in movement as to be able to catch flying birds with their paws.

Note 16. This is what the Two-Edged Sword Mountains are like!

In this range, the mountains are so high, the cliffs so precipitous, and the passes so few, that it was almost impossible to devise a means of crossing them. The Chinese, however, have invented an ingenious kind of pathway called a "terraced" or "flying" road. Holes are cut in the face of the cliffs, and wooden piles are mortised into them at an angle. Tree trunks are then laid across the space between the tops of the piles and the cliff wall, making a corduroy road, the whole being finally covered with earth. These roads are so solidly built that not only people, but horses and even small carts, can pass over them. As there are no railings, however, travel upon them is always fraught with more or less danger.

NOTES

LOOKING AT THE MOON AFTER RAIN

Note 17. Half of the moon-toad is already up.

In Chinese mythology, the *ch'an*, a three-legged toad, lives in the moon and is supposed to swallow it during an eclipse. The toad is very long-lived and grows horns at the age of three thousand years. It was originally a woman named Ch'ang O, who stole the drug of Immortality and fled to the moon to escape her husband's wrath. The moon is often referred to as *ch'an*, as in the poem.

Note 18. The glimmer of it is like smooth hoar-frost spreading over ten thousand li.

A *li* is a Chinese land measurement, equal to about one third of a mile.

THE LONELY WIFE

Note 19. There is only the moon, shining through the clouds of a hard, jade-green sky.

The term "jade," in Chinese literature, includes both the jadeites and nephrites. These semi-transparent stones are found in a great variety of colours. There are black jades; pure white jades, described by the Chinese as "mutton fat"; jades with brown and red veins; yellow jades tinged with green; grey jades with white or brown lines running through them; and, most usual of all, green jades, of which there are an infinite number of shades.

These green jades vary from the dark, opaque moss-green, very much like the New Zealand "green-stone," to the jewel jade called by the Chinese *fei ts'ui*, or "kingfisher feather," which, in perfect examples, is the brilliant green of an emerald. As a result of this range of

NOTES

colouring, the Chinese use the term "jade" to describe the tints seen in Nature. The colours of the sky, the hills, the sea, can all be found in the jades, which are considered by the Chinese as the most desirable of precious stones. In addition to its employment in actual comparison, the word "jade" is very often used in a figurative sense to denote anything especially desirable.

Note 20. Beneath the quilt of the Fire-Bird, on the bed of the Silver-Crested Love-Pheasant.

The Fire-Bird is the *Luan*, and the Love-Pheasant the *Fêng Huang*; both are fully described in the table of mythical animals in the Introduction.

Note 21. As the tears of your so Unworthy One escape and continue constantly to flow.

The term "Unworthy One" is constantly used by wives and concubines in speaking of themselves to their husbands or to the men they love.

Note 22. As I toss on my pillow, I hear the cold, nostalgic sound of the water-clock.

The clepsydra, or water-clock, has been used by the Chinese for many centuries, one can still be seen in the North Worshipping Tower in Canton, and another in the "Forbidden" portion of the Peking Palace, where the dethroned Manchu Emperor lives. The following account of the one in Canton is taken from the "Chinese Repository," Volume XX, Page 430: "The clepsydra is called the 'copper-jar water-dropper.' There are four covered jars standing on a brickwork stairway, the top of each of which is level with the bottom of the one above it. The largest measures twenty-three inches high and broad and contains seventy catties or ninety-seven and a half pints of water; the second is twenty-two inches high and twenty-one inches broad; the third,

NOTES

twenty-one inches high and twenty broad; and the lowest, twenty-three inches high and nineteen inches broad. Each is connected with the other by an open trough along which the water trickles. The wooden index in the lowest jar is set every morning and afternoon at five o'clock, by placing the mark on it for these hours even with the cover through which it rises and indicates the time. The water is dipped out and poured back into the top jar when the index shows the completion of the half day, and the water is renewed every quarter."

THE PLEASURES WITHIN THE PALACE

Note 23. From little, little girls, they have lived in the Golden House.

The "Golden House" is an allusion to a remark made by the Emperor Wu of Han who, when still a boy, exclaimed that if he could marry his lovely cousin A-chiao he would build a golden house for her to live in.

Palaces were often given most picturesque names, and different parts of the precincts were described as being of "jade" or some other precious material, the use of the word "golden" is, of course, in this case, purely figurative.

The organization of the Imperial seraglio, which contained many thousands of women, was most complicated, and the ladies belonged to different classes or ranks.

There was only one Empress, whose title was *Hou*, and, if the wife of the preceding monarch were still alive, she was called *T'ai Hou*, or Greater Empress. These ladies had each their own palace. Next in rank came the principal Imperial concubines or secondary wives called *Fei*. As a rule, there were two of them, and they had each their palace and household. After them came the *P'in* described as "Imperial concubines of first rank," or maids of honour, who lived together in a large palace

NOTES

and who, once they had attained this rank, could never be dispersed. (See Note 69.) The ladies of the Court are often spoken of as *Fei-P'in*. Of lower rank than these were the innumerable Palace women called *Ch'ieh*, concubines or handmaids. The use of the word is not confined to the inmates of the Palace, as ordinary people may have *ch'ieh*. Little girls who were especially pretty, or who showed unusual promise, were often sent to the Palace when quite young, that they might become accustomed to the surroundings while still children. (See Introduction.)

Note 24. They are lovely, lovely, in the Purple Hall.

The Ruler of Heaven lives in a circumpolar constellation called the Tzŭ Wei, Purple Enclosure; therefore the Palace of his Son, the Ruler of Earth, is called "Purple."

Note 25. Their only sorrow, that the songs and wu dances are over.

The wu dance is a posturing dance for which special, very elaborately embroidered dresses with long streamers are worn. As the arms move, these scarves float rhythmically in the air.

Note 26. Changed into the five-coloured clouds and flown away.

The allusion to the five-coloured clouds is to the beautifully variegated clouds, bright with the five colours of happiness, upon which the Immortals ride.

WRITTEN IN THE CHARACTER OF A BEAUTIFUL WOMAN

Note 27. Bright, bright, the gilded magpie mirror.

Magpies are the birds of happiness. There is an old story of the Gold Magpie which tells that, ages ago, a husband and wife, at parting, divided a round mirror between them, each keeping a half as a guarantee of fidelity. Unhappily, the wife forgot her marriage vows,

NOTES

and to her horror the half circle she had kept turned into a magpie and flew away. Since then, magpies are often carved on mirror backs as reminders and warnings.

Note 28. I sit at my dressing-stand, and I am like the Green Fire-Bird who, thinking of its mate, died alone.

The Green Fire-Bird is a fabulous creature who is regarded as the embodiment of every grace and beauty. It is the essence of the Fire God, and references to it in stories of love and marriage are frequent. One of the most popular of these tales is that of a King of India who caught a beautiful bird with green plumage of an extraordinary brilliance. He valued it greatly, and had an exquisite gold cage made for it. For three years it lived in captivity, and not a sound came from it in all that time. At last, the King, who was much puzzled at its silence, consulted his wife, saying: "Is the creature dumb?" She replied: "No, but every creature is the same, when it meets one of its own species it will speak." Not knowing how to obtain a mate for the Green Fire-Bird, the King placed a large mirror in its cage. The *Luan* danced with joy, uttered strange cries, and then, with all its strength, hurled itself against its own reflection and fell dead.

Note 29. My tears, like white jade chop-sticks, fall in a single piece.

It was said of the Empress Ch'ên of Wei (403–241 B.C.) that her tears fell so fast they formed connected lines like jade chop-sticks.

SONGS TO THE PEONIES

Note 30. The "Songs to the Peonies" were written on a Spring morning when Ming Huang, accompanied by Yang Kuei-fei, his favourite concubine, and his Court, had gone to see the blooms for which he had a passion. As he

NOTES

sat, admiring the flowers and listening to the singing of the Palace maidens, he suddenly exclaimed: "I am tired of these old songs, call Li Po." The poet was found, but unfortunately in a state best described by the Chinese expression of "great drunk." Supported by attendants on either side of him, he appeared at the pavilion, and while Yang Kuei-fei held his ink-slab, dashed off the "Songs." She then sang them to the air, "Peaceful Brightness," while the Emperor beat time.

The "Songs" compare Yang Kuei-fei to the Immortals and to Li Fu-jên, a famous beauty of whom it was said that "one glance would overthrow a city, a second would overthrow the State." But, unluckily, Li T'ai-po also brought in the name of the "Flying Swallow," a concubine of the Han Emperor Ch'êng, who caused the downfall of the noble Pan Chieh-yü (see Note 155) and is looked upon as a despicable character. Kao Li-shih, the Chief Eunuch of the Court, induced Yang Kuei-fei to take this mention as an insult, and it finally cost Li T'ai-po his place at Court.

In the third "Song," there is an allusion to the Emperor under the figure of the sun. When his presence is removed, the unhappy, jealous flowers feel as if they were growing on the North side of the pavilion.

Yang Kuei-fei, the most famous Imperial concubine in Chinese history, was a young girl of the Yang (White Poplar) family, named Yü Huan, or Jade Armlet; she is generally referred to as Yang Kuei-fei or simply Kuei-fei — Exalted Imperial Concubine.

The Chief Eunuch brought her before the T'ang Emperor, Ming Huang, at a time when the old man was inconsolable from the double deaths of his beloved Empress and his favourite mistress.

The story goes that the Emperor first saw Yang Yü Huan, then fifteen years old, as she was bathing in the

NOTES

pool made of stone, white as jade, in the pleasure palace he had built on the slopes of the Li Mountains. As the young girl left the water, she wrapped herself in a cloak of open-work gauze through which her skin shone with a wonderful light. The Emperor immediately fell desperately in love with her, and she soon became chief of the Palace ladies wearing "half the garments of an Empress."

Yang Kuei-fei rose to such heights of power that her word was law; she had her own palace, her own dancing-girls, and was even allowed by the doting monarch to adopt the great An Lu-shan, for whom she had a passion, as her son. Her follies and extravagancies were innumerable, and her ill-fame spread about the country to such an extent that, when the rebellion broke out (see Note 37), the soldiers refused to fight until she had been given over to them for execution.

After her death, Ming Huang spent three inconsolable years as an exile in Szechwan, and his first act upon his return to the Empire, which he had ceded to his son, was to open her grave. It was empty. Even the gold hair-ornaments, and the half of a round gold box shared with the Emperor as an emblem of conjugal unity, had gone; the only trace of the dead beauty was the scent-bag in which she had kept these treasures. "Ah," cried the unhappy monarch, "may I not see even the bones of my beloved?" In despair, he sent for a Taoist magician and begged him to search the Worlds for Yang Kuei-fei. The Taoist burnt charms to enlist the help of the beneficent spirits, but these were unsuccessful in their search. He finally sat in contemplation until the "vital essence" issued from his body and descended to the World of Shades. Here the names of all the spirits who have passed from the World of Light are entered in classified books, but that of Yang Kuei-fei was not among them.

NOTES

The demon in charge insisted that if the name were not entered, the spirit had not arrived, and the Taoist left, sad and crest-fallen.

He then reflected that if she really were not at the Yellow Springs below, she must be among the Immortals above. He therefore ascended to Paradise, and asked the first person he met, who happened to be the Weaving Maiden who lives in the sky, for news of the lost lady. The Weaving Maiden was most uncommunicative, and found much difficulty in believing that Ming Huang, who had consented to the execution of Yang Kuei-fei, really mourned her death, but finally admitted that she was living among the Immortals on the island of P'êng Lai in the Jade-grey Sea, and even assisted the Taoist to find her. She then told Yang Kuei-fei that, if she still loved the Emperor, the Moon Mother might be induced to allow a meeting at the full moon on the fifteenth day of the Eighth Month. Yang Kuei-fei eagerly assented, and giving the Taoist a gold hairpin and her half of the round box as a proof of her existence, begged that he hasten back to the World of Light and make all arrangements with her lover.

Accordingly, at the appointed time, the Taoist threw his fly-whip into the air, creating a bridge of light between this world and the moon, and over this Ming Huang passed. Yang Kuei-fei was waiting for him. She stood under the great cassia-tree which grows in the moon, and was surrounded by fairies.

The story, which is often sung to the air "Rainbow Skirts and Feather Collar," goes on to relate that the Weaving Maiden was moved to deep pity by their joy at meeting and arranged with the Jade Emperor, Chief Ruler of the Heavens, that the pair, immortalized by their great love, should live forever in the Tao Li Heaven.

NOTES

THE PALACE WOMAN AND THE DRAGON ROBES

Note 31. I ponder his regard, not mine the love
Enjoyed by those within the Purple Palace.

    The Palace woman of Ch'in was evidently one of the lower ranks of concubines who lived in the Women's Apartments and only appeared when sent for, not in one of the palaces given to ladies of higher rank.

Note 32. If floods should come, I also would not leave.
A bear might come and still I could protect.

    Now that she is no longer needed, she reflects sadly on the stories of two heroines whose behaviour she would gladly have emulated. These are Fên Chieh-yü, a favourite of the Han Emperor, Yüan, who once protected her master with her own body from the attack of a bear which had broken out of its cage; and Liu Fu-jên, concubine of King Chao of Ch'u. It is told of Liu Fu-jên that one day she went with the King to the "Terrace by the Stream," where he told her to wait for him until he returned from the capital. While she waited, the river rose, but she refused to leave unless by Imperial command. By the time this arrived she was drowned.

Note 33. Of serving Sun and Moon.

    The "Sun and Moon" are the Emperor and Empress.

THE NANKING WINE-SHOP

Note 34. In the wine-shops of Wu, women are pressing the wine.

    Wine made from grain is fermented for several weeks in tubs and then strained or "pressed" through cloths. It is not red, like wine from grapes, but either a shade of yellow or pure white. Wines made from grapes, plums, apples, pears, lichis, and roses, are sometimes used, but are not nearly so strong as the decoctions from grains.

NOTES

FÊNG HUANG T'AI

Note 35. *The silver-crested love-pheasants strutted upon the Pheasant Terrace.*

About A.D. 493, three strange and beautiful birds were noticed inside the city walls of Nanking, then called the "City of the Golden Mound." At first, the people did not suspect the identity of the birds, but when they saw that all the other birds assembled and appeared to be paying homage to the strangers, they realized that the visitors were the famous *Fêng Huang*. (See table of mythical birds in Introduction.) The terrace was built to commemorate the occasion.

Note 36. *Here also, drifting clouds may blind the Sun.*

The drifting clouds are supposed to be the evil courtiers who have poisoned the mind of the Emperor, i.e. the Sun, against Li T'ai-po.

THE NORTHERN FLIGHT

Note 37. The An Lu-shan rebellion, which broke out during the reign of the T'ang Emperor, Ming Huang, was very nearly successful, and, if the leader had not been assassinated in A.D. 757 by his son, might have caused the overthrow of the dynasty. As it was, the Emperor, having fled to Szechwan — a step strongly deprecated by Li T'ai-po in the poem, "The Perils of the Shu Road" (see Note 11) — abdicated in favour of *his* son, Su Tsung, who crushed the rebellion. The poem refers to the time when it was at its height, and the Emperor's forces were flying to the North.

Note 38. *The rushing whale squeezes the Yellow River;*
The man-eating beasts with long tusks assemble at Lo Yang.

During the rebellion, both sides of the Yellow River were

NOTES

lined with rebels, the population was obliged to fly, and the country was devastated as if a whale had rushed up the river and caused it to overflow its banks.

The "beasts" are fabulous creatures called *tso chih*, with tusks three feet long, who delight in eating the flesh of men. Li T'ai-po uses them metaphorically for the rebels who are threatening the capital.

Note 39. When, before our glad faces, shall we see the Glory of Heaven?
The Emperor, under the usual figure of the Sun.

THE CROSSWISE RIVER

Note 40. I say the Crosswise River is terrible.
The savage wind blows as if it would overturn the Heaven's Gate Mountains.

The "Crosswise River" is that section of the Yangtze which flows past steep cliffs in Anhwei. The "Heaven's Gate Mountains" tower above, making a sharp defile.

Note 41. From the beginning of things, the Ox Ledge has been more dangerous than the Standing Horse Hill.

A very swift current runs past the Ox Ledge, and boats are obliged to wait for daylight before attempting to breast it. The Standing Horse Hill, so called from its resemblance to a standing horse, is above a reach of the Yangtze where the river is comparatively tranquil.

Note 42. Is the Eighth Month tide-bore of Chêkiang equal to this?
The Ch'ien T'ang River in Chêkiang is famous for its bore, or tidal wave. During the autumnal equinox, this bore sometimes attains a height of twenty feet and more.

CH'ANG KAN

Note 43. I could not yet lay aside my face of shame;
I hung my head, facing the dark wall.

NOTES

In China, little girls are supposed to hide their faces at the suggestion of marriage.

Note 44. I often thought that you were the faithful man who clung to the bridge-post.

A certain Wei Shêng had a great reputation for sincerity and reliability, which was put to proof on an occasion when he had an appointment with a lady to meet on a bridge. The lady did not come. But, in spite of the fact that the waters rose to a flood, Wei Shêng would not leave. Finally, as he stood there clinging to the bridge-post to keep himself firm, the waves engulfed him and he was never seen again.

Note 45. That I should never be obliged to ascend the Looking-for-Husband Ledge.

A hill on the banks of the Yangtze, so called because of a legend that, many centuries ago, a wife, whose husband had been away for several years, went daily to watch for his returning sail. In the end, she was turned to stone on the spot where she had kept her vigil.

Note 46. To the Ch'ü T'ang Chasm and the Whirling Water Rock of the Yü River

Which, during the Fifth Month, must not be collided with;
Where the wailing of the gibbons seems to come from the sky.

The Ch'ü T'ang is the first of the three noted chasms in the upper reaches of the Yangtze. At the point where the River Yü empties into the Yangtze, there is a great rock which, when uncovered, is more than two hundred feet high. In the Fifth Month (June) the water from the melting snows of the Tibetan mountains causes the river to rise to such an extent that the rock is covered, which makes it especially dangerous to navigation. The height of the cliffs on either side of the gorge is so tremendous that the wailing of the gibbons (see Note 15) in the woods above sounds as though it came from the sky.

NOTES

*Note 47. I will not go far on the road to meet you,
  I will go straight until I reach the Long Wind Sands.*

      The Long Wind Sands are many a day's journey from the village of Ch'ang Kan, which stands just outside the South Gate of Nanking. What the lady implies is that she will go to "the ends of the earth" to meet her returning husband.

SORROW DURING A CLEAR AUTUMN

Note 48. I climb the hills of Chiu I.

      The Chiu I, or "Nine Peaks," lie to the South of the Tung T'ing Lake (see map) into which the three divisions of the Hsiang River debouch after having united.

Note 49. I go by the "Bird's Path."

      A term very often used for steep mountain paths.

Note 50. I think much of fishing for a leviathan from the Island of the Cold Sea.

      The legend referred to at the end of the poem is as follows: A group of five islands in the Pi Hai, the Jade-grey Sea, were inhabited by the Immortals, who found themselves very uncomfortable as these islands, instead of standing firmly, rose and fell in the most disconcerting manner. The Immortals therefore applied to the Jade Emperor for assistance, and he commanded fifteen leviathans, three to each island, to raise their heads and support the islands, thus keeping them from rocking. All was well until a man from the Elder Dragon Country appeared and with one cast of his line caught six of the monsters, the result being that two of the islands toppled over and sank in the sea. The three which remain are known as the "Three Hills of the Immortals." This tale has become proverbial, and people who are disappointed in their ambition say "I have no rod with which to catch a leviathan."

NOTES

POIGNANT GRIEF DURING A SUNNY SPRING

Note 51. I feel as one feels listening to the sound of the waters of the Dragon Mound in Ch'in.
(See Note 9.)

Note 52. The gibbons wailing by the Serpent River.
(See Note 15.)

Note 53. I feel as the "Shining One" felt when she passed the Jade Frontier,
As the exile of Ch'u in the Maple Forest.

Two allusions which suggest homesickness. The "Shining One" is Chao Chün. (See Note 79.) The exile of Ch'u is Ch'ü Yüan, the famous statesman. (See Note 62.)

TWO POEMS WRITTEN TO TS'UI (THE OFFICIAL)

Note 54. In both these poems, Ts'ui is compared to T'ao Yüanming, author of "Once More Fields and Gardens," published in this volume. T'ao is the ideal of the educated scholar, who prefers a life in the fields to any official post. Many stories are told of him. He planted five willows in front of his house, and is therefore often spoken of as the "Teacher of the Five Willows." He was so fond of music that he declared he could imagine the sweet sounds of the *ch'in*, and often carried about a stringless instrument over which he moved his hands. The *ch'in*, or table-lute, is fully described in Note 114.

WIND–BOUND AT THE NEW FOREST REACH

Note 55. To-day, at dawn, see the willows beyond the White Gate.

The White Gate is the Western Gate. The points of the compass are governed by colours, elements, mythological beasts, and seasons, thus:

East: Green. Wood. The Blue-green Dragon. Spring.

NOTES

South: Red. Fire. The Vermilion Bird. Summer.
West: White. Metal. The White Tiger. Autumn.
North: Black. Water. The Black Warrior. Winter.
Centre: Yellow. Earth.

DRINKING ALONE IN THE MOONLIGHT

Note 56. But we will keep our appointment by the far-off Cloudy River.
The Cloudy River is the Chinese name for the Milky Way.

Note 57. There would be no Wine Star in Heaven.
The Wine Star is a constellation composed of three stars, to the North of the Dipper.

Note 58. There should be no Wine Springs on Earth.
The Wine Springs lie, one in Kansu, and one in Shansi. (See map.) The water of the one in Kansu is supposed to taste like wine, that of the one in Shansi is used in the making of wine.

RIVER CHANT

Note 59. Jade flageolets and pipes of gold.
The Chinese flageolet is a tube measuring a little more than a foot in length. It has five holes above, one below, and one at the end through which it is played. They are now made of bamboo, but formerly were made of copper, jadestone, or marble, as such materials were considered less liable to be affected by the weather.

Note 60. The Immortal waited,
Then mounted and rode the yellow crane.
Tou Tzŭ-an, who had attained Immortality by living a life of contemplation, was transported to the Taoist Paradise by a crane so old that it had turned yellow.

NOTES

Note 61. Rather would he be followed by the white gulls.

This line refers to a story from a book treating of Taoist subjects long supposed to have been written by a philosopher called Lieh Tzŭ, but this is now known to have been a Second Century forgery. A translation of the story reads: "The man who lived by the sea loved the sea-gulls. Every day, as the sun rose above the horizon, the birds from the sea assembled in hundreds and flew about. His father said: 'I hear the sea-gulls follow you and fly round you. Catch some in your hands and bring them to me that I too may enjoy them.' The next day the birds from the sea all performed the posturing dance in the air, but did not descend."

Note 62. The tzŭ and fu of Ch'ü P'ing hang suspended like the sun and moon.

The *tzŭ* and *fu* are two irregular forms of verse, they are referred to in the Introduction in the part dealing with versification. Ch'ü P'ing is another name for Ch'ü Yüan, a famous poet and statesman who lived 332–295 B.C. (See Introduction.)

Note 63. I could move the Five Peaks.

The sacred mountains of the "four quarters" and the nadir (or the four points of the compass and the centre of the earth). They are the T'ai Shan in the East, the Hua Shan in the West, the Hêng Shan in the North, the Hêng Shan in the South, and the Sung Shan in the centre.

SEPARATED BY IMPERIAL SUMMONS

Note 64. The Emperor commands; three times the summons. He who left has not yet returned.

The official has not responded quickly to the summons from the capital, so the messenger has been obliged to come three times. Upon the third occasion, the official realizes that the matter is urgent and prepares to

NOTES

depart the next day at sunrise, before the messenger can have reached the Palace on his return journey.

Note 65. Our thoughts will be with each other. I must ascend the Looking-for-Husband Hill.
(See Note 45.)

Note 66. You must not imitate Su Ch'in's wife and not leave your loom.
Su Ch'in, who lived in the Fourth Century B.C., was away from home many years; when he returned, his wife took no notice whatever, and did not even leave the loom at which she sat weaving cloth.

A WOMAN SINGS TO THE AIR: "SITTING AT NIGHT"

Note 67. I sit, sit in the North Hall.
The "North Hall" is a term for the Women's Apartments, which always lie farthest from the Great Gate placed in the South wall of the house. (See Plan of House.)

Note 68. Then, though my Lord sang ten thousand verses which should cause even the dust on the beams to fly, to me it would be nothing.
It is said that when Yü Kung, a man of the State of Lu who lived during the Han Dynasty, sang, the sounds were so exquisite that even the dust on the beams flew. "To cause the dust on the beams to fly" has therefore become a current saying.

THE PALACE WOMAN AND THE SOLDIERS' COOK

Note 69. Once the Unworthy One was a maiden of the Ts'ung Terrace.
The Ts'ung Terrace referred to by the sad lady who, in the dispersal of the Palace women (see Introduction), had fallen to such a low degree, stood in the Palace of King Chao, who lived at the time of the "Spring and Autumn Annals," many centuries before our era.

NOTES

A BEAUTIFUL WOMAN ENCOUNTERED ON A FIELD–PATH

Note 70. Down comes the riding-whip, straight down — it strikes the Five Cloud Cart.
  The Immortals used Five Coloured Clouds to ride upon, therefore the term, "Five Cloud Cart," has become a complimentary expression for a cart or carriage in which a beautiful young woman is travelling.

HEARING A BAMBOO FLUTE IN THE CITY OF LO YANG

Note 71. I hear "The Snapped Willow."
  An allusion to the old song suggesting homesickness. (See Note 2.)

THE RETREAT OF HSIEH KUNG

Note 72. Hsieh Kung is the honorary title of the poet, Hsieh T'iao, who lived in the Fifth Century A.D. Li T'ai-po, who greatly admired him, constantly quoted his poems, and expressed a wish to be buried on the Spring-green Mountain where Hsieh Kung had lived. Some accounts say that he was first buried elsewhere, but that afterwards his body was removed and put where he desired.

A TRAVELLER COMES TO THE OLD TERRACE OF SU

Note 73. The old Imperial Park — the ruined Terrace — the young willows.
  Early in the Fifth Century B.C., Fu Ch'ai, King of Wu, built the Ku Su Terrace to please Hsi Shih, one of the most famous beauties in history. It was nearly two miles long, and took three years to build. Its foundations can still be traced on the hills near Soochow, which was the capital of Wu.

NOTES

THE REST-HOUSE ON THE CLEAR WAN RIVER

Note 74. I love the beauty of the Wan River.
A little river near Ning Kuo-fu in Anhwei. (See map.)

Note 75. Really, one cannot help laughing to think that, until now, the rapid current celebrated by Yen
Has usurped all the fame.
The philosopher Yen Kuang (*circa* A.D. 25) is better known as Yen Tzŭ-ling. The river in which he loved to fish was the Hsin An.

ANSWER TO AN AFFECTIONATE INVITATION FROM TS'UI FIFTEEN

Note 76. A party of friends who are in the habit of meeting each other constantly are called by numbers according to age. The same custom is used to distinguish members of a family. (See Introduction.)

Note 77. You have the "bird's foot-print" characters.
Writing is supposed by the Chinese to have been invented by Ts'ang Chieh, a minister of the Yellow Emperor (2698–2598 B.C.) who, having "observed the shapes of things in the heavens and the forms of things on earth, also the foot-prints of birds and beasts on the sand and mud," suddenly conceived the idea of pictographic writing. It is highly complimentary to speak of a person's writing as being like the "bird's foot-prints."

Note 78. You suggest that we drink together at the Lute Stream.
The Ch'in Ch'i T'ai (Table-lute Stream Terrace) was a stone terrace where a famous player of the table-lute, who is said to have attained Immortality, lived. The legend is that he took a small dragon in the form of a carp from the Ch'in stream and kept it for a month, when it changed its shape into that of a dragon and ascended to Heaven.

NOTES

THE HONOURABLE LADY CHAO

Note 79. Moon over the houses of Han, over the site of Ch'in.
Ch'in was the name of the State which overcame all the others and welded China into a homogeneous Empire instead of a loose federation. (See Introduction.) The lady Chao lived during the Han Dynasty.

Wang Ch'iang, known to posterity as Chao Chün, the "Brilliant-and-Perfect," lived in the First Century B.C. The daughter of educated parents, she was brought up in the strictest Confucian principles; in the words of the Chinese, she "did not speak loudly nor did she look beyond the doors, indeed, even within the house, she only walked the path which led to her mother's room. Her ears were closed to all distracting sounds, therefore her heart and mind were pure like those of the Immortals." Her father regarded her as a precious jewel, and although many suitors presented themselves, he refused to listen to their proposals, and finally, when she was seventeen, sent her to the capital as an offering to the Han Emperor Yüan.

Upon arriving at the Palace, the young girl was housed in the inner rooms, among the innumerable Palace women who lived there in constant hope of a summons to the Imperial presence. As the Son of Heaven never went into this part of his Palace, it was customary to catalogue the inmates and submit their portraits to him, a form of procedure which led to much bribery of the Court painters. The rigid principles of the daughter of the Wang clan forbade her to comply with this Palace custom, and the portrait which appeared in the catalogue was such a travesty of her exquisite features that it roused no desire in the Imperial breast.

Five or six dreary years passed, and the young girl remained secluded in the Women's Apartments. Shortly

NOTES

before this time, one of the Hsiung Nu tribes (see Note 3) had surrendered to the Chinese soldiers, and as a proof of good faith on both sides had received permission to serve as a frontier guard. Soon after, the head of the tribe sent to ask that one of Yüan Ti's ladies be sent him as Queen. The catalogue was consulted, and the decision fell upon the daughter of Wang as being the one among the Palace women who had the fewest charms. She was therefore told to prepare herself for a journey to the desert wastes where she would reign over a savage Central Asian tribe, a prospect terrifying to one brought up in strict seclusion among people of refinement.

Custom demanded that, on the point of departure, she should appear before the Son of Heaven in order to thank her Imperial Master for his kind thoughtfulness in thus providing for her future, and then be formally handed over to the envoys. The audience was held in one of the secondary halls, the Court was assembled, the envoys stood ready, and the lady entered. At the sight of her unusual beauty, every one was thunderstruck, even the Emperor could hardly refrain from springing off the Dragon Throne and speaking to her. But it was too late; there was nothing to be done. The most beautiful of all the Palace women was pledged to the Hsiung Nu Khan, the escort which was to convey her over the Jade Pass waited, and soon the broken-hearted girl set off.

Fury and consternation spread through the Palace; a camel laden with gold was sent in pursuit; the guilty painter, Mao Yen-shou, was executed and his immense fortune sent as a consolation to the Wang family; but all this could not save the young girl from her fate. The Hsiung Nu ambassador refused to ransom her, and she passed out through the Jade Barrier to the "Yellow Sand Fields" beyond.

The banished daughter of Han was true to the prin-

NOTES

ciples in which she had been schooled. Instead of committing suicide, as she longed to do, she submitted to the will of the Five Great Ones — Heaven, Earth, The Emperor, her Father, and her Mother — and performed her duties as a wife to the best of her ability in spite of the homesickness from which she suffered perpetually.

Upon the death of the Khan, she felt that her hour of deliverance had at last come and that she was at liberty to poison herself. This she did, and was buried in the desert, but the mound over her grave remained always green.

Because of her pseudonym, "Brilliant-and-Perfect," she is often referred to as "Ming Fei," the "Bright Concubine." Allusions to her story always suggest homesickness.

THINKING OF THE FRONTIER

Note 80. I desire to send the "harmonious writings."
Letters from wives to husbands are often spoken of as though they carried sweet sounds.

Note 81. He who wears the dragon robes delighted in the sweetly-scented wind of her garments.
Appointments for the Emperor's use were all spoken of as "dragon" appontments, and the analysis of the character which means the Emperor's love, is a dragon under a roof. Ladies' clothes were, and are to-day, kept in cupboards in which scented woods were burned, therefore as the long sleeves of their dresses swayed back and forth a sweet perfume came from them.

Note 82. How was it possible for the "Flying Swallow" to snatch the Emperor's love?
The "Flying Swallow" was a famous concubine. (See Note 30.)

NOTES

RECITING VERSES BY MOONLIGHT

Note 83. I suggest that men meditate at length on Hsieh Hsüan Hui.
   A reference, under a pseudonym, to the poet Hsieh T'iao, whose work Li T'ai-po so much admired. (See Note 72.) "Hsüan" is applied to the names of gods to indicate that they deserve praise and worship, and "Hui" means bright, splendid, or a ray of the sun.

PASSING THE NIGHT AT THE WHITE HERON ISLAND

Note 84. At dawn, I left the Red Bird Gate.
   An allusion to the bird which rules the South. (See Note 55.)

Note 85. At sunset, I came to roost on the White Heron Island.
   According to the Chinese commentary, this island lies "in the heart's centre of the river, three *li* West of the district of the Golden Mound (Nanking), and many herons collect there."

Note 86. And the longing in my heart is like that for the Green Jasper Tree.
   This tree grows in the Taoist Paradise, supposed to lie in the K'un Lun Mountains. (See map.) Those who eat its blossoms become immortal.

ASCENDING THE THREE CHASMS

Note 87. These are the famous chasms of the Yangtze River, between Ichang and Chungking. Their names are: "The Terrifying Barrier," "The Sorceress Gorge," and "The Western Sepulchre." Joined together in one great line of precipitous cliffs, they are among the extraordinary natural objects of the world and are most awe-inspiring.

NOTES

Note 88. The Serpent River runs terribly fast.
The Serpent River can be suddenly exhausted.
    A reference to the fact that, although the water of the river flows with terrible speed while the snow waters are coming down, during the Winter it is very low, and many parts are quite dry. (See Note 46.)

Note 89. Three dawns shine upon the Yellow Ox.
Three sunsets — and we go so slowly.
    A cliff beneath which are rapids so difficult and dangerous to pass that the utmost care must be taken in navigating them. Boats ascending this stretch of the river often take several days to pass a given point. (See Introduction for a description of the Yangtze River and travel upon it.)

PARTING FROM YANG, A HILL MAN

Note 90. You are going to pick the fairy grasses
And the shooting purple flower of the ch'ang p'u.
    "Hill men" is a term applied to those who desire to become worthy of joining the ranks of the Immortals, and for this reason lead a life of contemplation among the hills. The fairy grasses and the *ch'ang p'u* (see table of plants in Introduction) both grow in the Taoist Paradises.

Note 91. Riding down from the green-blue Heaven on a white dragon.
    The dragon is one of the steeds of the Immortals.

THE SERPENT MOUND

Note 92. The mercy of the Sainted Lord is far greater than that of Han Wên Ti.
The Princely One had pity, and did not appoint you to the station of the Unending Sands.
    The allusion is to an incident which occurred in the

NOTES

Second Century B.C. when a famous scholar named Chia was sent to Ch'ang Sha, literally "Unending Sands" (see map), and died there of the damp vapours.

ON THE SUBJECT OF OLD TAI'S WINE-SHOP

Note 93. Old Tai is gone down to the Yellow Springs.
> The Yellow Springs lie in the nether world, where spirits go after death.

Note 94. There is no Li Po on the terrace of Eternal Darkness.
> This world is known as the World of Light, and below it lies the World of Shades, where the sun never shines.

DRINKING IN THE T'AO PAVILION

Note 95. The garden pool lies and shines like the magic gall mirror.
> The Magic Gall Mirror was a square of glittering, polished metal supposed to possess the miraculous power of betraying the thoughts of all who looked into it, by making the heart and "five viscera" visible. The ferocious First Emperor used it to examine his numerous Palace women, and those who, by a palpitating gall, showed lack of faith were put to death.

Note 96. The Golden Valley is not much to boast of.
> A beautiful garden built by the rich and eccentric Shih Ch'ung (died A.D. 300) for his favourite concubine Lü Chu.

A SONG FOR THE HOUR WHEN THE CROWS ROOST

Note 97. This is the hour when the crows come to roost on the Ku Su Terrace.
> (See Note 73.)

Note 98. The silver-white arrow-tablet above the gold-coloured brass jar of the water-clock marks the dripping of much water.
> (See Note 22.)

NOTES

POEM SENT TO THE OFFICIAL WANG OF HAN YANG

Note 99. The shrill notes of the bamboo flute reached to Mien and O.
Mien and O are the ancient names for Hankow and Wuchang.

DRINKING ALONE ON THE ROCK IN THE RIVER OF THE CLEAR STREAM

Note 100. Perpetually casting my fish-line like Yen Ling.
Yen Ling is one of the names of the philosopher Yen Kuang. (See Note 75.)

THE REST-HOUSE OF DEEP TROUBLE

Note 101. At Chin Ling, the tavern where travellers part is called the Rest-House of Deep Trouble.
An inn fifteen *li* South of the district in which Chin Ling (Nanking) stands.

Note 102. Like K'ang Lo I climb on board the dull travelling boat.
K'ang Lo is a pseudonym for the poet Hsieh Ling-yün, who lived in the Fifth Century A.D.

Note 103. I hum softly "On the Clear Streams Flies the Night Frost."
A line from one of Hsieh Ling-yün's poems.

Note 104. It is said that, long ago, on the Ox Island Hill, songs were sung which blended the five colours.
The "five colours" are blue-green, yellow, carnation, white, and black. Anything that is perfectly harmonious is spoken of figuratively as being blended like the five colours.
Rapids flow past the Ox Island Hill on the Yangtze, which is not to be confused with the Ox Hill at the Yangtze Gorges.

NOTES

Note 105. Now do I not equal Hsieh, and the youth of the House of Yüan?

Yüan Hung lived in the time of the Chin Dynasty. His poems were both erudite and beautiful, but his extreme poverty forced him to take a position on a freight-boat plying up and down the Yangtze. One night, as the vessel lay below the dangerous Ox Rapids waiting for daylight, the official of the place, a learned man named Hsieh Shang, heard Yüan Hung's exquisite songs and was so delighted that he insisted upon the singer's accompanying him to the Official Residence. Here the days and nights were passed in conversation, and upon Yüan Hung's departure, Hsieh gave him much silver and gold, and eventually used his influence to enable the young man to become an official. Since then all men have heard of Yüan Hung. Li T'ai-po compares his lonely lot to that of the youth who possessed a faithful friend.

Note 106. The bitter bamboos make a cold sound, swaying in the Autumn moonlight.

The ancient Chinese divided bamboos into two classes: the bitter and the tasteless.

THE "LOOKING-FOR-HUSBAND" ROCK

Note 107. In the attitude, and with the manner, of the woman of old.

A reference to a legend of a woman who was turned to stone. (See Note 45.)

Note 108. Her resentment is that of the Woman of the Hsiang River.

O Huang and her sister Nü Ying were the wives of Shun, the "Perfect Emperor" (2317–2208 B.C.). When he died, and was buried near the Hsiang River, they wept so copiously over his grave that their tears burned spots on the bamboos growing there, and thus was the variety

NOTES

known as the "spotted bamboo" created. Eventually the despairing ladies committed suicide by throwing themselves into the river.

Note 109. Her silence that of the concubine of the King of Ch'u.

Ts'u Fei, concubine of the King of Ch'u, was much distressed because her lord was of a very wild disposition, and only took pleasure in hunting and such pursuits. She constantly expostulated with him on his mode of life, but at last, finding that all her entreaties were in vain, she ceased her remonstrances and sank into a silence from which she could not be roused.

AFTER BEING SEPARATED FOR A LONG TIME

Note 110. Besides there are the "embroidered character letters."

In the Fourth Century A.D., a lady, whose maiden name was Su, embroidered a long lament of eight hundred and forty characters in the form of a poetical palindrome and sent it to her husband who was exiled in Tartary.

BITTER JEALOUSY IN THE PALACE OF THE HIGH GATE

Note 111. The Heavens have revolved. The "Northern Measure" hangs above the Western wing.

The "Northern Measure" is the Chinese name for the "Dipper," and on the fifteenth day of the Eighth Month, when it can be seen sinking in the West before bed-time, a festival is held. This is essentially a festival for women, who object to being parted from their husbands at that time. Incense is burned to the full moon, and many fruits and seeds, all of a symbolical nature denoting the desire for posterity, are set out for the moon goddess.

Note 112. In the Gold House, there is no one.

(See Note 23.)

NOTES

ETERNALLY THINKING OF EACH OTHER

Note 113. The tones of the Chao psaltery begin and end on the bridge of the silver-crested love-pheasant.

"The *sê*, or psaltery, is made on the principle of the *ch'in*, and like that instrument has been made the subject of numerous allegorical comparisons. The number of strings has varied ... but the *sê* now in use has twenty-five strings. Each string is elevated on a movable bridge. These bridges represent the five colours: the first five are blue, the next red, the five in the middle are yellow, then come five white, and lastly five black." ("Chinese Music," by J. A. Van Aalst.) The most desirable specimens came from Chao, a place in Shensi. (See map.) The allusion to the love-pheasants is, of course, symbolical. By it, the lady says that this instrument is only properly used for love-songs, with the implication that it is therefore impossible for her to play it now.

Note 114. I wish I could play my Shu table-lute on the mandarin duck strings.

The *ch'in*, or table-lute, lies on a table like a zither, and is played with the fingers. It is " one of the most ancient instruments, and certainly the most poetical of all ... The dimensions, the number of strings, the form, and whatever is connected with this instrument had their principles in Nature. Thus the *ch'in* measured 3.66 feet, because the year contains a maximum of 366 days; the number of strings was five, to agree with the five elements; the upper part was made round, to represent the firmament; the bottom was flat, to represent the ground; and the thirteen studs stood for the twelve moons and the intercalary moon. The strings were also subjected to certain laws. The thickest string was composed of two

NOTES

hundred and forty threads and represented the Sovereign." ("Chinese Music," by J. A. Van Aalst.) The "Shu table-lute" is an allusion to Ssŭ Ma Hsiang-ju, a great poet and musician, who was a native of Shu. The mandarin ducks are emblems of conjugal love, and in speaking of them the wife expresses the wish that her husband were present to listen.

Note 115. *I wish my thoughts to follow the Spring wind, even to the Swallow Mountains.*

The Yen Jan, or "Swallow Mountains," lie several thousand miles to the West of Ch'ang An, in Central Asia.

Note 116. *The neglected lamp does not burn brightly.*

The lamps were little vessels filled with natural oil, upon which floated a vegetable wick. Unless constantly attended to, and this was the duty of the woman, the flame was small and insignificant.

SUNG TO THE AIR: "THE MANTZŬ LIKE AN IDOL"

Note 117. The Mantzŭ are an aboriginal tribe still living in the far Southwest of China. It was here that Li T'ai-po was to have been exiled had not the sentence been commuted. (See Introduction.)

Note 118. *Instead, for me, the "long" rest-houses alternate with the "short" rest-houses.*

On the "great roads," which we should speak of as paths, rest-houses for the convenience of travellers are erected every five *li* (a *li* is one-third of a mile). These are called "short road rest-houses" and are simply shelters. There are also "long road rest-houses" every ten *li*, where the care-takers serve travellers with tea and food, and which are equipped with altars and idols for the convenience of the pious.

NOTES

AT THE YELLOW CRANE TOWER, TAKING LEAVE OF MÊNG HAO JAN

Note 119. I take leave of my dear old friend at the Yellow Crane Tower.
 Mêng Hao Jan (A.D. 689–740) was a very famous poet, one of whose idiosyncrasies was riding a donkey through the snow in a search for inspiration.
 The Yellow Crane Tower is still standing at Wuchang. (See map and Note 60.)

THOUGHTS FROM A THOUSAND LI

Note 120. Li Ling is buried in the sands of Hu.
 Li Ling lived during the reign of the Emperor Wu of Han (140–87 B.C.) at a time when the Hsiung Nu tribes were very troublesome. He penetrated far into the Hsiung Nu country, with a force of only five thousand infantry, and was there surrounded by thirty thousand of the enemy. After his men had exhausted their arrows, he was forced to surrender, and spent the rest of his life as a captive in Central Asia.

Note 121. Su Wu has returned to the homes of Han.
 Su Wu lived during the same period as did Li Ling, and was sent by the Emperor Wu upon a mission of peace to the Hsiung Nu. By the time he reached the Court of the Khan, however, relations between the Chinese and the Barbarians were again strained, and he was taken prisoner. Various attempts were made to induce him to renounce his allegiance to China; he was thrown into prison and subsisted for days on the moisture which he sucked from his clothes, but all efforts to undermine his loyalty failed, and eventually he was sent to tend sheep on the grazing fields of the steppes. Years passed, Wu Ti, the "Military Emperor," died, and his successor

NOTES

Chao Ti made peace with the Central Asian tribes and sent envoys to ask for the return of the faithful Su Wu. The Khan replied that he was dead, but the envoy was able to answer that such could not be the case, as, not long before, the Emperor himself while hunting in his park had shot a wild goose, and had found a letter from Su Wu tied to its leg. The loyal official was therefore sent back to China. He had gone off in the prime of life; when he returned, in 86 B.C., he was a broken-down, white-haired old man.

Note 122. *Wild geese are flying.*
If I sent a letter — so — to the edge of Heaven.
An allusion to the story of Su Wu. Letters anxiously awaited are often spoken of as "wild-goose" letters.

SAYING GOOD-BYE TO A FRIEND WHO IS GOING TO THE PLUM-FLOWER LAKE

Note 123. *I bid you good-bye, my friend, as you are going on an excursion to the Plum-Flower Lake.*
This lake lies about seven miles Southwest of Nanking. The legend is that, many years ago, a raft loaded with flowering plum-trees sank in it, and ever since, during the plum-blossom season, the lake is covered with plum-trees in bloom.

Note 124. *Nevertheless you must not omit the wild-goose letter.*
(See Notes 121 and 122.)

Note 125. *Or else our knowledge of each other will be as the dust of Hu to the dust of Yüeh.*
Hu is the Mongols' country to the North and West of the Great Wall, and Yüeh is the province of Chêkiang in the Southeast of China. (See map.)

NOTES

A DESULTORY VISIT TO THE FÊNG HSIEN TEMPLE AT THE DRAGON'S GATE

Note 126. I had already wandered away from the People's Temple.
The Fêng Hsien is one of the so-called Chao Ti temples. These temples are erected by the people, not by Imperial command, which fact is proclaimed on an inscription written on a horizontal board placed over the main doorway. The Fêng Hsien temple stands in the Lung Mên, or Dragon Gate, a defile cut in the mountains of Honan by the great Yü when he drained the Empire about two thousand B.C. (See Introduction.) He is supposed to have been helped by a dragon who, with one sweep of its tail, cleft the mountain range in two, thus forcing the river I, a confluent of the Lo which is one of the tributaries of the Yellow River, to confine itself within the defile through which it runs in a series of rapids.

CROSSING THE FRONTIER — II

Note 127. Sadness everywhere. A few sounds from a Mongol flageolet jar the air.
The Hsiung Nu soldiers, against whom the Chinese are fighting, are so near that the sounds of their flageolets can be plainly heard.

Note 128. Perhaps it is Ho P'iao Yao.
(See Note 4.)

AT THE EDGE OF HEAVEN. THINKING OF LI T'AI-PO

Note 129. The demons where you are rejoice to see men go by.
The demons are of the man-eating variety, the *yao kuai*.
(See table of supernatural beings in Introduction.)

Note 130. You should hold speech with the soul of Yüan.
Ch'ü Yüan (see Note 62) drowned himself in the Mi Lo River.

NOTES

SENT TO LI PO AS A GIFT

Note 131. And remembering Ko Hung, you are ashamed.
Ko Hung, author of "Biographies of the Gods," lived in the Fourth Century A.D. Although very poor, he pursued his studies with such zeal that he became an official. Having heard that the cinnabar, from which the Elixir of Immortality is distilled, came from Cochin China, he begged to be appointed to a magistracy in the South in order that he might obtain a supply for experimental purposes on the spot. Arrived in Kwangtung, he spent his time on Mount Lo Fo attempting to compound this elixir, and so, working at his experiments, passed into a tranquil sleep. When his friends went to wake him, they found his clothes empty. Ko Hung had ascended to the Taoist Paradise to live forever among the Immortals.

HEARING THE EARLY ORIOLE

Note 132. The sun rose while I slept. I had not yet risen.
The poem alludes to the curious Chinese custom of holding Imperial audiences at dawn. This custom was persisted in until the fall of the Manchu Dynasty in 1912. One of the most noticeable peculiarities of Peking in Imperial days was the noise during the night, which never seemed to stop. Officials came to the Palace in their carts, while it was still dark, in order to be ready for the audience at dawn. It is clear from Po Chü-i's poem that he is no longer in office, since, although the sun has risen, he himself is still in bed.

AN IMPERIAL AUDIENCE AT DAWN

Note 133. At the first light of the still-concealed sun, the Cock-man, in his dark-red cap, strikes the tally-sticks and proclaims aloud the hour.

NOTES

The Cock-men, whose badge of office was a red cloth, were in charge of the water-clock, and their business was to announce the time of day. Near the water-clock were kept bamboo tallies, one for each division of the twenty-four hours. (See Introduction.) When the arrow of the water-clock registered the moment of the change from one division into another, the Cock-man on duty struck the appropriate tally-stick on a stone set for that purpose beside the door of the Palace. At sunrise, which took place during the hour of the monkey (three to five A.M.) or during the hour of the cock (five to seven A.M.), according to the season, he gave a loud, peculiar cry to warn the inmates of the Palace that day had come.

Note 134. At this exact moment, the Keeper of the Robes sends in the eider-duck skin dress, with its cloud-like curving feather-scales of kingfisher green.

The "Keeper of the Robes" was one of the six offices instituted by the Ch'in Dynasty (255–209 B.C.), the other five were those of the "Imperial Head-dresses," "Food-stuffs," "Washing Utensils," "Sitting Mats," and "Writing Materials." Robes were, and are, made from the skins of the various eider-ducks found in Northern Asia. The king eider's head is blue; the Pacific eider's, black and green; while the spectacled eider has a white line round the eye, which accounts for its name. The feathers are so close and soft that garments made of them feel exactly like fine fur.

Note 135. In the Ninth Heaven, the Ch'ang Ho Gate opens.

The Ninth Heaven is the centre from which the points of the compass radiate, and it is there that the first of all the entrances to Heaven, the Ch'ang Ho Gate, stands.

Note 136. The immediately-arrived sun tips the "Immortal Palm."

The "Immortal Palm" was a very tall bronze pillar

NOTES

which the Emperor Wu of Han erected in the grounds of the Variegated Colours Palace. On the top was a colossal hand, with the fingers curled up so that the falling dew might be caught in the palm, for, of course, the ancient Chinese firmly believed that dew fell. As dew was the drinking-water of the Immortals, to drink it was to advance a step on the road to Immortality. The hand was brightly polished, and was one of the first objects about the Palace to glitter when the sun rose.

SEEKING FOR THE HERMIT OF THE WEST HILL

Note 137. On the Nothing-Beyond Peak, a hut of red grass.
Huts were built of a certain hill grass, now very rare. It turns red in the Autumn, and is fine and strong like wire.

Note 138. I look into the room. There is only the low table and the stand for the elbows.
Much of the furniture in the T'ang period was like that used now by the Japanese. It was customary to sit on the floor and write at a low table, and the use of the elbow-stand was general.

Note 139. I have received much — the whole doctrine of clear purity.
The principles of Taoism are called literally "the clear pure doctrines."

Note 140. Why should I wait for the Man of Wisdom?
An allusion to the eccentric Wang Hui-chih (A.D. 388), who made a long journey through the snow to see a friend, but missed him.

FAREWELL WORDS TO THE DAUGHTER OF THE HOUSE OF YANG

Note 141. The sacredness with which the Chinese regard their family ties is well known, but it is perhaps not realized

NOTES

that the Chinese conception of the duties owed to friendship entails very great responsibilities. If a friend dies, it is a man's duty to see that his family do not suffer in any way. Wei Ying-wu is probably addressing the daughter of some dead friend whom he has brought up in his own family, or she may be a poor relation on his mother's side, but that she is not his own daughter is clear from the fact that her clan name differs from his, which is Wei.

ONCE MORE FIELDS AND GARDENS.

Note 142. But for thirteen years it was so I lived.
  The text reads "three ten," which is the way the Chinese say "thirty," but native commentaries state that it should read "ten three," or thirteen. This is far more in accordance with the facts of T'ao's life. He lived A.D. 365-427, and although he became an official, he soon resigned his post, saying that he "could not crook the hinges of his back for five pecks of rice a day." (See Note 54.)

Note 143. Mine is a little property of ten mou or so.
  A *mou* is a Chinese land measurement which is equal to about one-sixth of an acre.

SONG OF THE SNAPPED WILLOW

Note 144. A very famous song written during the Liang Dynasty (A.D. 502-557). Allusions to it always suggest homesickness

THE CLOUDY RIVER

Note 145. There seems to be no doubt that although King Hsüan of Chou (876-781 B.C.) is not mentioned by name in the poem, which appears in the "Decade of Tang" division

NOTES

of the "Book of Odes," he is the King referred to. All the old Chinese commentators agree in ascribing the authorship to a certain Jêng Shu, an officer of the Court during the reign of that monarch, who is known to have had a profound admiration for the King. Opinions differ as to the exact date of the great drought, but the standard chronology places it in the sixth year of King Hsüan's reign, 821 B.C. This ode illustrates the Chinese conception of kingship described in the Introduction.

Note 146. How the Cloudy River glitters.
> The Chinese call the Milky Way the "Cloudy" or "Silver River." Stars are peculiarly bright and glittering during a drought.

Note 147. My stone sceptres and round badges of rank.
> The badges of office were made of nephrite. There are references in both the "Book of History" and the "Book of Odes" to the fact that, after certain sacrifices, they were buried in the ground. In this case, the sacrifices had been performed so often that the supply of these tokens was exhausted.

Note 148. I myself have gone from the border altars to the ancestral temples.
> According to Confucius, the sacrifices to Heaven and Earth were performed at the border altars, and those to the ancestors took place at the temples especially provided for the purpose.

Note 149. Hou Chi could do no more.
> Hou Chi is the deity of grain, and from him King Hsüan was supposed to be descended.

Note 150. Shang Ti does not look favourably upon us.
> Shang Ti, literally the "Above Emperor," is the supreme ruler of the universe. Earthly Emperors receive the decree which empowers them to rule from him.

NOTES

Note 151. *Why should I not be terrified*
Since all the ancestral sacrifices will be ended?
  To the Chinese, this is the greatest calamity that can be conceived, since without these sacrifices the ancestral spirits would suffer greatly, and might visit their wrath upon their descendants.

Note 152. *Drought, the Demon of Drought, has caused these ravages.*
  The "Book of Spirits and Prodigies" states that in the Southern regions there is a hairy man, two or three cubits in height, with eyes in the top of his head and the upper part of his body bare. His name is Po. He runs with the speed of the wind, and in whatever part of the country he appears a great drought ensues.

Note 153. *I offered the yearly sacrifices for full crops in good time.*
  It was the custom for the King to pray and make offerings to Shang Ti during the first Spring month (February), in order to propitiate this chief of the Chinese pantheon and ensure good harvests from the grain then being sown. During the first Winter month (November), other prayers and sacrifices were offered to the "Honoured Ones of Heaven" (the sun, moon, and stars) for a blessing on the year to follow.

Note 154. *I neglected not one of the Spirits of the Four Quarters of the Earth.*
  Sacrifices of thanksgiving to the "Spirits of the Four Earth Quarters" were offered at the end of the harvest season.

SONG OF GRIEF

Note 155.   Pan Chieh-yü, the talented and upright concubine of the Han Emperor, Ch'êng, is one of the ladies most often referred to in literature. She was supplanted by the beautiful, but unscrupulous, "Flying Swallow," who accused her to the Emperor of denouncing him to the

NOTES

kuei and the *shên*. (See table of supernatural beings in Introduction.) The Emperor, therefore, sent for Pan Chieh-yü who, kneeling before him, answered him as follows: "The Unworthy One of the Emperor has heard that he who cultivates virtue still has not attained happiness or favour. If this be so, for him who does evil what hope is there? Supposing that the demons and spirits are aware of this world's affairs, they could not endure that one who was not faithful to the Emperor should utter the secret thoughts hidden in the darkness of his heart. If they are not conscious of this world's affairs, of what use would the uttering of those secret thoughts be?" Then, rising, she left the Imperial presence, and immediately obtained permission to withdraw from the Palace. Not long after, she sent the Emperor "A Song of Grief," and ever since then the term, "Autumn Fan," has been used to suggest a deserted wife.

LETTER OF THANKS FOR PRECIOUS PEARLS

Note 156. One of the ladies swept aside by Yang Kuei-fei (see Note 30) was the lovely Chiang Ts'ai-p'in, known as the "Plum-blossom" concubine. As she liked to differ from other people, she painted her eye-brows in the shape of wide cassia-leaves instead of the thin-lined willow-leaf, or "moth-antennæ," the form so much used. Soon after her departure from the Palace, some pearls were received as tribute, and the Emperor, who still had a lingering regard for "Plum-blossom," sent them to her in secret. She refused the pearls, and returned them to the Emperor with this poem.

SONGS OF THE COURTESANS

Note 157. I gaze far — far — for the Seven Scents Chariot.
The "Seven Scents Chariot" was a kind of carriage used

NOTES

in old days by officials, and only those above the sixth rank might hang curtains upon it. It was open on four sides, but covered with a roof. The hubs of the wheels were carved. Ai Ai implies that the person she is waiting for is very grand indeed.

THE GREAT HO RIVER

Note 158. This song, which was probably written about 600 B.C., has been elucidated by succeeding generations of Chinese commentators in the following tale.

The lady was a daughter of the Lord of Wei, and the divorced wife of the Lord of Sung. On the death of her husband, her son succeeded to his father's position as feudal chief of Sung. Because of her divorce, the unhappy woman, who was deeply attached to her son, was forbidden to enter Sung, where he lived.

AN EVENING MEETING

Note 159. The lamp-flower falls.

An old-fashioned Chinese lamp was simply a vessel in which a vegetable wick floated in oil. If the oil were very pure, the wick burned evenly, leaving no charred end; but if the oil were impure, the wick turned red-hot and formed a glowing tip called the "lamp-flower." Its appearance was looked upon as the happy omen which foretold a lover's speedy return.

Note 160. But what is the rain of the Sorceress Gorge.

The Sorceress Gorge (see Note 87) is often referred to in a figurative sense, as it is in this poem. The allusion is to the story of a certain prince who dreamed that a fairy, calling herself the Lady of the Sorceress Mountain, came and passed the night with him. On leaving in the morning, she told him that it was she who ruled over the

NOTES

clouds and rain, which would ever after be symbols of their love. Since then, the expression "clouds and rain" has become a euphemism for the relation of the sexes.

CALLIGRAPHY

Note 161. The writing of Li Po-hai.
  Li Yung (A.D. 678–747) is often called "Po Hai" in reference to a place where he held office. He was a person who displayed astounding knowledge at a very early age, and rose to be very powerful. When he was nearly seventy, he was overthrown by the machinations of his enemies and put to death. He wrote many inscriptions and was noted for his beautiful, spirited calligraphy.

Note 162. The writing of Chia, the official.
  Chia K'uei (A.D. 30–101) was known as the "Universal Scholar." He was an eminent teacher, and many of his pupils came from great distances. As the payment he received was in grain, he was said to "till with his tongue," which phrase has now become a current expression for earning one's living as a teacher. Toward the end of his life, he was appointed Imperial historiographer. He was also a noted calligraphist. (See Note 77.)

ONE GOES A JOURNEY

Note 163. Are many sweet-olive trees.
  The *olea fragrans,* or sweet-olive, is employed in a metaphorical sense to denote literary honours. Scholars who have successfully passed their examinations are said to have gathered its branches.

ON THE CLASSIC OF THE HILLS AND SEA

Note 164. Because the Yellow Emperor considers them of importance.

NOTES

The Yellow Emperor is one of the five mythical sovereigns who ruled *circa* 2697 B.C. and is supposed to have reigned a hundred years.

THE SOLITARY TRAVELLER

Note 165. He has attended an Imperial audience at the Twelve Towers.
The "Twelve Towers" was a palace built by Ming Huang (see Note 30) for the use of his ladies. It was an attempted imitation of a building supposed to have been erected by the Yellow Emperor (see Note 164) for the use of the Immortals. By his reference to it, one knows that the traveller has been to Court and is returning disappointed.

SPRING. AUTUMN. WINTER

Note 166. It makes me think
Of the Peach-Blossom Fountain.
An allusion to a well-known allegory, "The Peach-Blossom Fountain," by T'ao Yüan-ming. (See Note 142.) It tells how a fisherman, who was lost, found himself in a beautiful country where the people all wore strange clothes of very old-fashioned cut. On coming home, he told many stories about this enchanting land, but it could never be found again. The gods had permitted the fisherman to return for a short time to the "peach-blossom" days of his youth, although he could never remember the road he had taken, nor even point out the direction in which it lay.

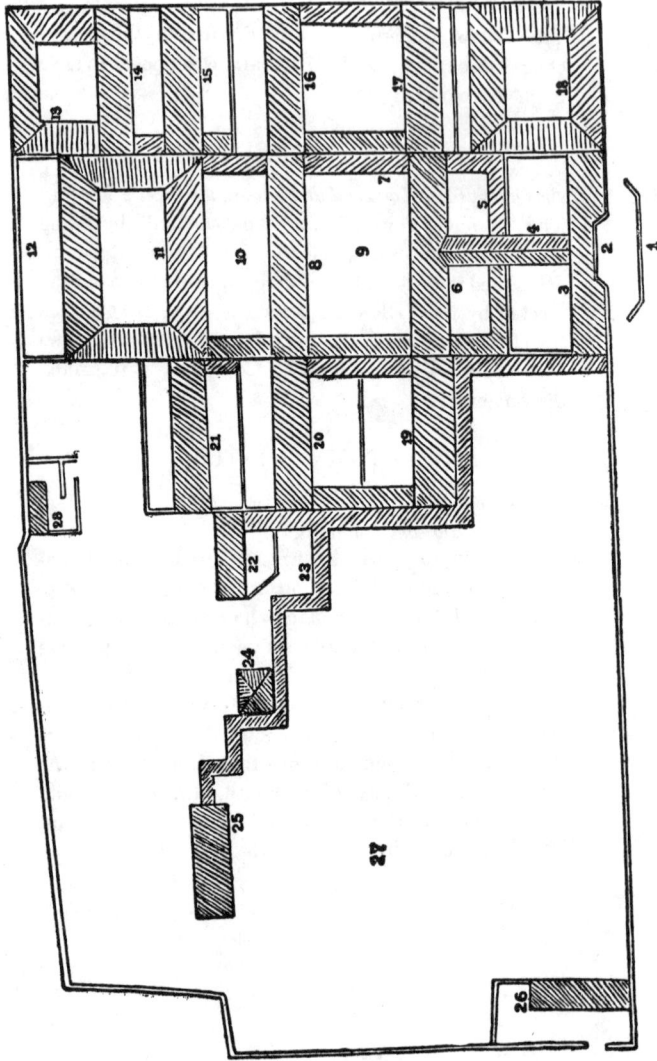

PLAN OF A TYPICAL CHINESE HOUSE OF THE BETTER CLASS

KEY TO PLAN OF A TYPICAL CHINESE HOUSE OF THE BETTER CLASS

Shaded Sections — Buildings.
White Sections — Courtyards.

The house faces South.

No. 1. Chao Pi.	Spirit Wall. Built to protect the main entrance from the malign influence of evil spirits: these move most easily in a straight line and find difficulty in turning corners, therefore a wall before the Great Gate is an effective defence.
No. 2. Ta Mên.	Great Gate.
No. 3. Mên Fang.	Gate-keeper's Room.
No. 4. Ting Tzǔ Lang.	Covered passage leading from the Reception Hall to the Great Gate and opening on the street.
No. 5. Lang.	Covered passage-way.
No. 6. T'ing.	Reception Hall.
No. 7. Lang.	Covered passage-way.
No. 8. T'ing.	Inner Reception Hall.
No. 9. Ch'ih.	A stone-paved courtyard. It has no roof and is raised in the centre. On great occasions, such as weddings, birthdays, and so on, it can be roofed and floored, thus being made a part of the house. Trees and flowers are not planted in this court, but are set about in pots.
No. 10. T'ing.	A courtyard. In this second courtyard, to which steps lead down, trees and flowers are planted, making of it an inner garden.
No. 11. Tso Ma Lou.	Running Horse Two-Story Apartments.

KEY TO PLAN OF A TYPICAL CHINESE HOUSE

	This is the *Kuei* so often spoken of, the Women's Apartments. It is a building in which the rooms surround a courtyard, and are connected by verandahs running round the court upstairs and down. The space in the centre is known as *T"ien Ching* or Heaven's Well. There are eighteen rooms in the upper story, and eighteen in the lower. The wife uses the front rooms; the daughters, the back.
No. 12. Hou T"ing.	Back Court. It is bounded by a "flower wall," or brick trellis, through which flowers can twine, and is used by the inmates of the *Kuei* as a garden.
No. 13. Nü Hsia Fang.	Women's Lower House. A house for the women servants. As in the house for men servants, No. 18, the floor is actually on a lower level than those of the master's apartments.
No. 14. Fo Lou.	Buddhist Two-Story Apartments. In the upper story, images of Buddhas, and of Kuan Yin, the Goddess of Mercy, are kept. As a rule, it is locked, and only people who have washed carefully and put on clean clothes may enter.
No. 15. Tsê Shih.	Side Inner Apartment. In this house, poor relations may live. The concubines who do not enter the *Kuei* except on invitation also live here. Guests do not go further into the house than to the wall bounding this building on the South.
No. 16. Tung Hua T"ing.	Eastern Flower Hall.
No. 17. Tui T"ing.	Opposite Hall. This and No. 16 are used for theatrical entertainments. The guests are seated in No. 16, facing South, and the

KEY TO PLAN OF A TYPICAL CHINESE HOUSE

	stage faces North in No. 17. A cloth covering is stretched over the courtyard, and a wall divides the two *T'ing* from the rest of the house.
No. 18. Nan Hsia Fang.	Men's Lower House. A house for men servants divided as far as possible from the quarters of the women servants, also placed conveniently near the Great Gate where guests enter.
No. 19. Ta Shu Fang.	Great Book Room. This room is used as a library and study, and in it the teacher instructs the sons of the family.
No. 20. Hsi Hua T'ing.	Western Flower Hall. Here guests are entertained at meals. Flower gardens are placed on either side, and also walls which prevent either the study or the women's rooms from being seen from it.
No. 21. Tsê Shih.	Side Inner Apartment. A building used by the ladies of the house as a study or boudoir, where they embroider, paint, or write. The light is very good, whereas in the *Kuei*, on account of most of the windows opening on the court ("Heaven's Well"), it is apt to be poor.
No. 22. Ch'u Fang.	Kitchen. This is placed conveniently near to No. 20, where the men of the family dine, and No. 21, the dining-room of the ladies.
No. 23. Ch'ü Lang.	Passage-of-Many-Turnings. The superstitious belief in regard to the difficulty experienced by evil spirits in going round sharp corners governs the planning of this strangely shaped passage.
No. 24. Shu Chai.	"Books Reverenced." The study, or students' room.

KEY TO PLAN OF A TYPICAL CHINESE HOUSE

No. 25. Hsien.   A Side-room or Pavilion. This is a long, low, outdoor passage, where guests sit and amuse themselves.

No. 26. Ma Fang.   Stable. The stable is placed as far as possible from the house. The horses, however, are kept saddled near the Great Gate for a large part of the day, in order to be in readiness should they be needed.

No. 27. Hua Yüan.   Flower Garden. The gardens are arranged with hills, water, and rockeries, to look as much like natural scenes as possible.

No. 28. Ssŭ So.   Privy.

TABLE OF CHINESE HISTORICAL PERIODS

Five Legendary Emperors.	2852–2205 B.C.
Hsia Dynasty.	2205–1766 B.C.
Shang Dynasty.	1766–1122 B.C.
Chou Dynasty.	1122–255 B.C.
Ch'in Dynasty.	255–206 B.C.
Han Dynasty.	206 B.C.–A.D. 25
Eastern Han Dynasty.	A.D. 25–221
Later Han Dynasty.	A.D. 221–264
Chin Dynasty.	A.D. 264–420
Period of Unrest, Six Short-lived Dynasties.	A.D. 420–618
T'ang Dynasty.	A.D. 618–906
The Five Dynasties:	A.D. 906–960
Posterior Liang.	
Posterior T'ang.	
Posterior Chin.	
Posterior Han.	
Posterior Chou.	
Sung Dynasty.	A.D. 960–1277
Yüan Dynasty.	A.D. 1277–1368
Ming Dynasty.	A.D. 1368–1644
Ch'ing Dynasty.	A.D. 1644–1912
Min Kuo (Republic of China).	A.D. 1912